WHY COME TO SLAKA?

MALCOLM BRADBURY is a well-known novelist, critic and academic. He set up the famous creative writing department of the University of East Anglia, whose students have included Ian McEwan and Kazuo Ishiguro. He is the author of seven novels: *Eating People is Wrong* (1959); *Stepping Westward* (1965); *The History Man* (1975), which won the Royal Society of Literature Heinemann Prize; *Rates of Exchange* (1983), which was shortlisted for the Booker Prize; *Cuts* (1987); *Doctor Criminale* (1992); and *To the Hermitage* (2000). He has also written several works of non-fiction, humour and satire, including *Who Do You Think You Are?* (1976), *All Dressed Up and Nowhere to Go* (1982) and *Why Come to Slaka?* (1991). He is an active journalist and a leading television writer, responsible for *Porterhouse Blue* (Channel 4), *Cold Comfort Farm* (BBC TV), many TV plays and episodes of *Inspector Morse*, *A Touch of Frost*, *Kavanagh QC* and *Dalziel and Pascoe*. He lives in Norwich, travels a good deal, and was awarded a knighthood in the year 2000.

Malcolm | Bradbury

Why Come to Slaka?

PICADOR

First published 1986 by Martin Secker & Warburg Ltd

This edition published 2014 by Pan Books
an imprint of Pan Macmillan, a division of Macmillan Publishers Limited
Pan Macmillan, 20 New Wharf Road, London N1 9RR
Basingstoke and Oxford
Associated companies throughout the world
www.panmacmillan.com

ISBN 978-1-4472-7221-2

A CIP catalogue record for this book is available from
the British Library.

Typeset by SetSystems Ltd, Saffron Walden, Essex

WHY COME TO SLAKA?
A Guidebook and a Phrasebook

TRANSLATED INTO ENGLISH BY DR F. PLITPLOV

(Dozent Extraordinarius, Universitet Dvarfim Borism)

INTRODUCTION BY DR A. PETWORTH

ISSUED BY THE MIN'STRATII KULTURI KOMIT'ETIII
(MUN'STRATUU KULTURU KOMUT'ETUUU)

PUBLISHED BY THE STATE PUBLISHING HOUSE 'V. I. LENINIM'
(PRAV'DI V. I. LENINSKI/PRAV'DU V. U. LENUNSKU)

PEOPLE'S REPUBLIC OF SLAKA
(STATII PRO'LETANIII SLAKAM/STATUU PRO'LETANUUU SLAKAM)

CONTENTI

Information on Weighs, Measures, Healths etc. etc. are dissipated through this book: somewhere there are maps and typical photographies.

WHY GO TO SLAKA?

Slaka!!!
Where is the heart that does not high upleap at the very merest
name of your immemorable city! Slaka!!! city of flours and
gipsy musick, of great buildungs and fine arts, we toast you in
your own brandy-spiritus!! Slaka!!! great city at the international crossroads, where for centuries people of the most
various parts have liked to come together for congress. Slaka!!!
bustling metropole of traders and entrepreners, where one time
a year exhibitionists of worldwide fame foregather in your great
halls of conference in most festivating mood for the justly
renowned 'Once-A-Year Commercial Travellers' World Fair'.
Slaka!!! sweet city of musicality and song, trios and filharmonias, where each summer the most prodigious musicians of all
lands come to perform in amazing fashions at the honoured
'Z. Leblat Musicology Festivi', the highest point of everyone's
musical dairy. Slaka!!! cosmopolite capital and shop-walker's
paradise!!! where in your noble bulevars pricey shops offer at
bargainous prices the very best of everythings. Slaka!!! duel of
the crown of of our favoured country, where the best heritages
of old times and the the contemporary charms of socialistical
cooperation meld to composite a lifestyle both antiquated and
progressive. Slaka!!! city of all-sorts, where in wondrous and
orgiastic mixtures the rationalistic clarities of the North meet
the boisterous intemperances of the South, the techniks of the
West meet the relaxing lethergies of the East, and everyone is
delighted! Slaka!!! capital of chic, so when nights descend and
the motor-cars swatch on our brightly lightered boulevards,

only a short stroll in this fine old town will convince you at a start there is much to be had.

Slaka!!! with your fine sepulchres and your rectorates of baroque accretion, who cannot smell everywhere your history? Slaka!!! with your laughing boys and your imping girls, who cannot want to delight in your happy people's? Slaka!!! with your exotic plates and your nightlife of the chicest kind, who can deny your pleasurabilities? Slaka!!! city which has captivated the soul and bodies of so many of all the ages, who can ever oblivate you?

Slaka!!! Oh, why do I not go there pronto?

How to Utilitate this Book

This book contains everything you need to survive in Slaka.
It is:
***Guidebook: with pictures of cities; maps of streets!!!
***Phrasebook: in probable situations and familiar usages, we show you how to master us linguistically. One look and you will see how simplified our language really is!!!
***Dictionary: how we list all our major nouns, verbs and other participles. Remember: we use both Cyrillies and Romanesque alfabetz, but for you we are Romanesque only?!!

MESSAGE FROM THE SLAKAN
HEAD OF STATE,
COMRADE-GENERAL I. VULCANI

Comrade Tourists!!!
In Slaka, when we drink, we like always to make toast. Our favourite toast is 'to dialogi!' With 'dialogi', we mean many things. 'Dialogi' is the friendship of all pease-loving fraternal peoples. 'Dialogi' is the great spirit of amity and concorde. 'Dialogi' means the desire for true intercurse – an intercurse where each parter is an equal and no one is on top! Now, in the mood of 'dialogi', I like to wellcome all turstiis, from here and there, from wherever and who knows, to the ambiant airs of our romantikal country. We wellcome you indisiscrimatly, from the friendly socialistical republics and from the imperialistic-fascist western powers, gladly recieving all nations and taking all currences! You will find our people warm to host you! See their arms, stretched out to greet you!! See their faces, smiling to meet you!! See their loins, girded to the task of giving you pleasure!! Know our motto: please come to us, and we promise, one day we will come to you!!
The land you wellcome to is a nation proud of its socialistik emulations. You will find our peoples marching bravely forward with their eyes ficked on the horizon of the future, their hands meanwhile baldly undertaking the works needed to achieve it. Everywhere you will find great and startling projets. We do not mind to make a criticism. In the past mistakes have been made, but we do not mention them. Certain errors have been committed, but now we correct them. In Slaka today, not all is perfet, but allmost. You will find here a land of noble achievements and fantastikal promises. And remember, for us even your

3

vacancy is a contribution! Last year a toto of 400,000 turstiis visited Slaka. This year our heroic travel-workers have pledged a new target: 500,000 plus turstii!! We know you like to help them brake their records!!

We summons you to come, asking only you observe our customs, as we like always to observe yours. We ask that you do not come with long hairs, if a man, or short, if a woman; this offends the modesse of our people and we cannot admit you. We ask also that you do not make a drunkness in public, except on our many state holidays, listed later on in this book. Obey please our kind laws and you will truly say, having wunderful time! Comrade turstiis, in Slaka we belief in travel, as a true striving for knowledge. If you come here, remember you do not take only holidays: you advance the brotherhood of nations and the cause of history. Of course you will also find some very nice beeches, and take home an excellent needleworks!!

By way of contusion, I extend my comradely embrace to those whose hard labors bore forth this book. I mention our great Min'stratii Kulturi Komit'etiii, who concieved this great projet under the wise new dirigation of our notable Culture-Minister F. Tankic; our National Academy of Arts and Sciences, whose excellent historical advisements were directed by Hero-Academician Dr Professor Rom Rum; our national-hero publishers and printers of the state press-house 'V. I. Leninim', whose redactive achievements are everywhere manfusted here; our culture-hero translator Dr F. Plitplov, whose prodigious interpretational facilitations made passable this Englisch-language edition; and our many fine travel-workers who exist only to turn your turstii dream into harsh reality.

Comrade-General I. Vulcani

INTRODUCTION

By Doktor Angus Petworthim
(Lektor in Linguistics, Bradford, England)

Not long ago, in the course of my professional duties (I lecture on the English language as a medium of international communication), I was invited to visit the fascinating Eastern country of Slaka. I am an experienced traveller who has lectured extensively for the British Council and can claim to have had diarrhoea for that excellent organization in most parts of the globe. It had however long been a matter of regret that I had never visited Eastern Europe, a place of fascination for me as for most Westerners. As for Slaka, I have to confess that I had never heard of it, thought it was somewhere quite different, and had never identified it on the map. This, perhaps, is not surprising, since it has frequently not been on it, having been often occupied by one or other of its nearer or further neighbours. Happily this ignorance was soon to be dispelled.

For, by great good fortune, I received an official letter from the Min'stratii Kulturi Komit'etiii of the People's Republic asking me to undertake a lecture tour in their land. The Min'stratii – the state cultural organization, for which the term 'Arts Council' would be a profoundly inadequate translation – would be my hosts and arrange my journey. Naturally I accepted at once. The visit that followed was, to say the least, unusual, and I regard it as one of the more amazing and indelible experiences of my life. To the Min'stratii I remain grateful for the spirited hospitality they afforded me – all the more generous since, owing to some small bureaucratic confusion, they were expecting a quite different Dr Petworth to come and lecture on a quite different topic. For three weeks I travelled in the country, not simply visiting universities, but going everywhere I liked (except of course in the restricted areas), seeing everything I cared to (apart, naturally, from materials of strategic importance) and meeting everyone I wanted (except, inevitably, in their own homes). To this day I recall the heavy savour of Slakan life, and the piquant texture of its political existence. I can truly say that a surprise awaited me round every corner, and I found myself captivated wherever I went.

What made this trip a journey I am never likely to forget? From the moment I stepped out of the flashy modern impermanence of Heathrow Airport into the COMFLUG plane (COMFLUG is of course the Slakan state airline) I felt my tour would be different. They tell us that mass travel has made the whole world much the same; if so, Slaka was clearly to be an exception. Where Western airlines obscure the discomforts and aggressions of travel with plastic food, bad films, strong drinks and fixed smiles from swollen-ankled stewardesses, COMFLUG with its wooden seating offered an immediate feeling of getting back to life's basics. That impact of the hard, sturdy roots of experience was to last throughout my tour, as I walked through Slaka's fine people's parks, inspected its great highrise developments of workers' apartments, toured its modern steelworks and its collective state farms, and saw the determined spirit of progress proclaimed on its banners everywhere. Despite the somewhat complicated currency rules (foreigners must change so much a day, to allow them to take advantage of the excellent export products, like the notable bottled beetroot and the incomparable brown shoes), and the difficulties of the language, even for an expert like myself, I feel I came to know the country, and it came to know me.

I also, I think, came to know its delightful people. It can surely be said that in no country is the Western visitor better watched over, and nowhere are there so many people who seem solely concerned for his or her interests and needs. Slaka is a land where no one need feel lonely or neglected, and those who think attentive hospitality is a lost art would be well advised to visit it. In the public buildings, the parks, the cafés, I made innumerable new friends, who pursued me wherever I went. Some courteously asked about the people I had met or intended meeting, offering all the help they could in identifying them. Others affectionately tried to help any transaction I might desire to undertake, generously asking if I cared to sell them my clothes, meet their female relatives, or engage in the various tradings and exchanges that are a kind of sport in this bantering and bartering land. With typical Slakan good nature they constantly asked for my autograph, took my address, and loaded me with introductions and messages for their relatives in other countries. So warm-hearted were they that there were times when I thought they would never let me go. The feeling of their affectionate attention still persists, and indeed explains why I am privileged to introduce this delightful book, so effectively rendered into his typically brilliant English by my old and demanding friend Dr F. Plitplov, presently Dozent Extraordinarius of Glit's renowned Boris the Small University, a leading Slakan translator, and a most vigorous international correspondent.

What shall I say about this fine volume? Like any regular traveller I have always felt dependent on having first-rate guides – ideally ones that are well organized, truly informative, neatly shaped, easily handled, not difficult to open or use, and instinctively ready to satisfy all one's most urgent needs. Indeed on my visit to Slaka, I was fortunate to have two of these. One, provided by the Min'stratii, was a most pleasant young lady, who acted as my interpreter, travelled everywhere with me, did all she could to display to me the mysterious face of her country, and even saved my life on a couple of occasions. I remain deeply in her debt. The other, equally helpful in its own more inanimate way, was this very book – or rather, not quite this very book, since it did not have a preface by me, for at that time I had not been there, and could not have been prevailed upon to write one, but an earlier edition, now, since it contains a good many outdated facts and figures (one of them the previous head of state, ~~Professor Vlad'mir Wanko~~), quite out-of-print. Thanks to various small changes that have lately taken place in the country (many of them occurring, as it happens, during my visit), a new edition, purging all previous errors, has proved necessary. This work, undertaken by the great state publishing house V. I. Leninim, now brings only totally accurate information, and I am delighted to participate in this, to use the Slakan phrase, great and startling project.

In these pages you will find everything needed to facilitate your journey to and in Slaka, and even out again. Like my own more human guide it will assist you linguistically and in every other way through every situation you are likely to encounter. Unlike her, it slips easily into the pocket. It has many uses, as tourist guide, detailed phrasebook and, in the waterproof edition, as a bathplug. It affords valuable information on almost everything: the problems of obtaining a visa, finding a hotel room, mastering the intricacies of the complex Slakan railway system, shopping, getting out of the various small confusions that arise on any holiday or business trip, and displaying the fascinating life and landsape of a country infinitely rich in this and not at all lacking in that. I am particularly pleased to see included an account of the Z. Leblat's great opera *Vedontakal Vrop*, having been fortunate enough to attend that work's modern revival, after it had been lost for 200 years. I recall with pleasure the evening I sat through that famous five-hour performance in Slakan, and can honestly say that its tale of comic confusions, mistaken identities and sexual chaos is one of the great expressions of the depth and interest of Slakan culture.

If you do intend to visit Slaka, this guide can be warmly recommended as quite incomparable (indeed, it is the only one). It can be recommended quite as warmly if you are *not* going to Slaka. In my book *The English Language As a Medium of International Communication* (University of Watermouth Press, 1981; reissued with corrections, 1986), I have occasion to remark that the world is structured like a language, and language is structured like a world. And – like those American menus so

8

mouthwateringly descriptive of the meal to come that they can almost be eaten instead of it, and are frequently rather better done – this book similarly could be said to be a verbal visit to Slaka in itself. Thus if you should not be able to make an actual visit to Slaka – and flights there are, it is true, not frequent, visas sometimes hard to obtain, travel arrangements, despite the efficient facilities of the state tourist board COSMOPLOT, sometimes complicated, and the language difficult, so that despite my own professional expertise I was unable to master it, even subsequently – this book could be an effective substitute. Indeed these delightfully produced pages may be said to contain almost everything about Slaka that can possibly be known.

But do not let reading this book deter you from making a visit. Slaka, as the guidebook says, is not to be missed. If the journey is hard, the compensations are many. The welcome is indeed warm, the atmosphere contemporary, and you can be truly promised a different kind of holiday. The food is pleasant, the drink excellent (especially the famous peach brandy, *rot'vitti*, which is definitely not to be missed!), the girls are pretty, especially after the drink, and so, it is said, are the men, especially after the girls. The artistic achievements are considerable, if sometimes baffling. Many fine buildings survive from ancient times, though I do not recommend the Cathedral, which is a long way out of town, inconveniently down by the River Nyit, and appears to be used as a place of unfortunate assignations. However, the tomb of the great liberator Grigoric affords a far more modern and comfortable place of pilgrimage. The state glass-blowing industry is well worth a visit, as are the fine museums of socialist achievement. Slaka is a great commercial capital, and you will find its great streets always lined with shoppers, keenly awaiting the arrival of some splendid new commodity. For any adventurous holidaymaker, Slaka offers a truly different and more up-to-date kind of holiday, and despite its extraordinary attractions it remains relatively uncrowded with fellow travellers. Velki in Slaka, the Slakans like to say, and, if you are like me, you will find yourself velki indeed. Vy'aggii boyo, da!!!

GEOGRAPHY AND HISTORY

By Professor-Academician Rom Rum
(Slakan Academy of Arts and Sciences)

SLAKA: WHERE IS?

Imagine please a beatiful small country from a fairytale, where on each high cragtop stands an ancient castello and in fine rustic residences the traditionally dressed pheasants of folklore plie away at their rural trades and practice their ancient customs, and dances by pheasants in regional costumes are regularly performed. Then please imagine also a paradisial workers' state, where the best principles of socialistic emulation guide advance into the future and agro-industry progresses appace with the willing cooperation of all. Now please put together one with the other these two fine imaginings, both pittoresque and progressive. What do you have? Perhaps you think, an unattainable paradise? Ignoramus!!!, it is not so! What you have is fact not a dream. Of course, it is the People's Republic of Slaka (Statii Pro'letanayii Slakam), which you should not neglect to visit.

Set by the generous hand of prodigious Mother Nature in a warm and wooded declivity between the delightful Vronopian mountains, truly we have in the city of Slaka just the kind of place where everyone likes to come. With the great Storkian plain to the east and the rolled hills of Pritprip to the west, fecundly watered by the great river Nyit which floods its proudish way throughout our verdant country, our famous city may fairly be called, in Dante's own evocative word, a 'paradiso'. Beyond spreads natural wonders and our great small cities, ancient and modern, blessed each in their own ways. Consider our wethers, neither Northern neither Southern. Here in beneficent circumstances the warm zephyrs of the Mediterranean meet the fine mistrals of Siberia to produce our famous laughing climat, sweetly warming in summers and bracingly colding in winters. Little wonder that at every season tourists in many numbers come to enjoy us, and of course we like to enjoy them.

And truly has so smiling been Nature's lavish hand that Slaka may claim all the geophysological advantages. Favoured by gaps in the great bandchain of mountainous ridges of Mittle Europe, offering all the vantage of river crossing from East and West or even vice verse, our land is the historical fountainhead of all the great trading routs. Equidistantly placed between the Baltic and the Adriatic, the Danube and the Blub, Slaka itself may still properly claim its ancient title as the central city of the universe. Stretched out as they are between norther plain and Alpine mont, alluvial plantain to sea-girt salted coast, our peoples may think themselves truely favoured. To them belongs a heritage of variousness. A land of infinite variables and unpredicted contrastables, the Slakan People's Republic may claim to be the melting pot of all human life. Here the oriental caravanseri of the great Silk Roads with their accompanies of Tartar hoards made their way to the westward, to encounter the Crusader armies of the West. In consequences, here was war and trade. Here scimitar struck blunderbum, and spice and silk traded for manufactured tricket and mechanistic geegaw. Known as 'the cultured crossroads', and also 'the bloody battlefield (tol'sto'ii incard'ninu) of Middle Europe', Slaka may count itself fortunate, not to say lucky, for what has been done it.

Such heritage still mirks Slaka today. As if the spirit of the Hunnish Atilla has met the romantic sole of middle Europe, the genii of Kublai Khan met with the essence of Martin Luther to create a rare people, fraught with the best weight of innumberable traditions. Truly our culture is a *pot pourri*, our heritage a salad. Over time our borders have been wide, small, and often not there at all. Today it is often said that our country is in a place quite differing from the place it started. Our faiths and loyalties have in the past been mixed, our languages many. Can

11

such variety be made as one country, united in one progressive cause?

The answer is, yes!!, or, as we have it, da da!! Today under the secure guidance of the Praesidium of the People's Republic, and with the wise wings of the USSR ever cast watchfully over us, Slaka shows everywhere its metal. Our peoples are united as one. Our borders of 1,200 vlodim are guaranteed to us, except in emergence. Our natural resources of beetroot and tin (how well one goes in the other!) are secondary to none. Home to the stork and the barbary goose, our terrains produce envious surplices. Industry does not neglect: our steel-production leaps by bounds.

SLAKA: HOW WAS?

Over generations historians and scholars have chittered and raged over Slakan history, but accurate facks are scarce and perplexiculities abound. Born far ago in the darkest ians of time, nurtured in the soul of that primeval forest which cradled all human life and kultur, to this day, history in Slaka is a mistery! No good recordings exist before Century X. The chronicle of Nostrum, famous monk of Kiev, believes our people were born first in the Bosphorus, but even such is dispute. Everywhere in Slaka we find human deposits which indicates our people have primitive origins. Our hero-archeologists find constant troves of primeval character, indicating the presents of hunter-wanderers. But who they were and what they were up for, which they hunted and why they wandered still is not evident. We know the incursive wondering tribes of the steppelands (the notorious Mogul hoards) came here, and there is not doubt that our Slakan salad has been flavoured by a Tartar source. Yet other tribes of the rape and pillage kind can also lay claim to the privilege of discovering the wonderful lands of Slaka. Medes and Swedes, Asians and Thracians, Tartars and Cassocks, Mortars and Turds clearly settled our terrain of lake and forest. All have left their imprint, their customs, and their jeans. This

Peasant youth with famous plums

shows clearly in the physical character of our peoples, who, you will find, are fair in the upper part and dark in the lower. And this explains too why in our natures you will find always a little bit of the Caucasian and a little bit of the Arrabesque!!

Today diggers of all kinds keep on upearthing bits of our pluralistic heritance. What is clear is that our paganistic times were interrupted – in Century IX, or possibly IIX, or X – by the comings-and-goings of Christianity. Legends tell that this was brought to Slaka by the former Comrade Patron-Saint of the country, Valdopin (??3–??8) but even these datums are oscure! Story tells that Valdopin came from either Byzantium or Constantinople to convert our tribals to the Christian heresy, and for a time succeeded. In consequences our land was recognized by the Holly Sea and became first a nation, beginning her great advance forward into the future of history. Alas not so Valdopin! He went on to convertate the paganistical tribals to the north, or the west, or maybe the south or just possibly the east, though this is particularly strongly disputed. By them he was tortued, massaced, and minced by swords into very fine pieces. Our Slakan fourbears liked to give him a marter's burial, and

13

requested the fine-chopped corse. A famous legend tells that a bargain was made in the Slakan fashion. The pieces of corse were set on one scale, measurated against an equal weigh of gold in the other. But all the gold of the Slakan treasor was piled and still that scale did not like to tipple!! Then came an old woman and set down her lively savings, a tiny coin!! Now did the scales tipple, and Valdopin's corse came to Slaka. The Domo of Saint Valdopin, now triumphantly restorated after bombings by our progressive architects, remains still by the waters of the River Nyit, but the sight is inassessible. Many church propagandas were made of this legend, and in past times when our people were deluded by religious values pilgrims came there often to repair their sights or throw away their cruches. Today the interpretations of socialistick materialist science explain the correct meaning of the story. Now it is recognize as a major folkish legend displaying that power belongs never to those rich and spoiled princies but to always to the people. Today our modern pilgrims preferate to visit the tombo of our great warrior-liberator of Marxist-Leninism, V. Grigoric. Yet we do not deny our Valdopin-legend. Certain it is that from that data forward, our Slakan peoples have always had a great love of exchange!!

So was our nation founded, but alas in following saecula history was not always so very kind to us. In the later millenaria constant sackings, pillage-and-rapings, invasions and external oppressions ocured: the dark-age of the history of the Slakan people. False prancelings and margraves dominated the land, nominated by our compressors. A succession of Transylvanian princes, Ottoman mamelukes, Teutonic nights and bishops-kratokrator swayed over us. In one reign only, under the bastard king Kermit the Indeterminate, our country was occupied no less than eighteen times by different foreign oppressors, while Kermit sat on his trone looking this way and that. No wonders then that over these times our morals declined. Our oppressors brought many faiths, and made our people swear. Our churches fell into neglect and wolves made their houses there. Our people leaders were cut down without ruth. Our learning halted and our langue fell to decline. No wonders then that few records of our dark age exist. Only one traveller of these times left an impression. The famed British tourer, Sir Fyffe Ffiennes, did reach in 1608 to Slaka, and recorded of his travellings: 'Wondrouf it if, that peoplef fhould have fettled here, there being here no wellf, no fuelf, no building ftuff of any kind to be efpied, and little for any to do fave confume their domeftick animalf. No artf of any kind are cultivated fave a form of dominoef, and mufik if alone the baggepyppef.'

Yet it if faid that the refourcy fluidneff of the Slakan character was forged by such evenements, so not all was bad. Famous oppressors emerged, as Boris the Short, who married Marie-Theresa the Fat, successored by his yet worse son, Quasimodo the Square. He liked to take our women to his castle and put our men to death down wells, unlike his son, Ladslav the Pretty, whose preference was opposite. Not until century XVIII did come a great cultural revival under Bishop 'Wencher' Vlam, whose castello still stands on top of Slaka today, and whose baroque tendencies are everywhere apparent in the city architectonics and the depravities of his court-life. Nudish masques were danced before the alters, and eunuchs performed in the streets. Today we may forgive some of these depravities because of Vlam's love of the arts. He nominated many musicians to haunt his courtings, including Z. Leblat, our great composer, who united the songing of folk and court, and is awarded if posthumously the title of First People's Artist for his unexcelling achievements.

Not however till the national arisering of century XVIX, led by Prince Bohumil the Shy, did our people seek a relief from oppression. In 1848 when all peoples of the region defiantly raised the banner of national liberations, the Slakans were not absent. Their gallant army of 350 men arose to throw off the yoke of the Turks, the Greeks, the Slovaks, the Prussians, the Swedes, the Piedmontese, the Serbs and the Gipsies. This united all nations against them, and in a heroical fight of twenty minutes they were bravely defeated. This great evenement was celebrated by our national poet-hero V. Hrovdat, killed on his horse as he very quickly receipted in battel his great 7,000-line epic poem *Rambo Flambo*. Since that time, our nation continued to alleagure with countries and protective alliances of all kinds, but always in the interests of our decadent burgois gentry and never in favour of the workers.

But as modern times rose it was clear that great evenements were on the iffing. Founded in 1910, the Slakan Workers' Party brought the vanguards of socialistikal thinkings to our country. Our great leader Grigoric, top-scoring student of Moscova in the 1920s, whose tombo we venerate in Plaz'scii P'rtyii, raleighed all enlightened souls under the slogo, 'Struvo vitam novam' (Strife for a new life). The scared-to-death landlording classes did not however budge, and a World War was required to release the promises of the great Comitern. During the war our peoples fought heroically on several sides, and numberous marble plaques dedicated to those who fell in national struggle remind us of those heroic days. In 1944 as the war concluded

Senathus of Hrovdat Universitet

Grigoric began a great workers' purge and liberated us to the fraternal Soviet army, and Slaka was proclaimed 'a people's republic'. Veritably here was a new day of dawning, and the peasants willingly gave up their lands and the house-owners their properties in their lust to become tools of hsitory. Truly Slaka today has proved by its creative application of the principals of Marxism-Leninism that all can contribute to concrete historical reality.

ACHIEVEMENTS AND POLITICAL SYSTEM

By Min'strat I. Tankic
(Minister of Culture)

SLAKA: WHO RUNS?

Today Slaka is a People's Republic belonging proudly to the fraternal brotherhood of socialistical societies and dedicated to the advance of history everywhere. Member of Warsava Pact and Comecon, loyal peas-loving 'brother in arms' of the URSS, it is a socialistic state of the working people of the country, run by the outstanding representatives of the proletariat class. Modern Slaka proudly boasts three political parties – the Slaka People's Communist Party (SPCP), the People's Slakan Communist Party (PSCP), and the Communist Slakan People's Party (CSPP). All have no difficulty to agree on the same progressive policies. If necessary, elections are frequently held, their victors often afforded the opportunity of entering government offices. Nowhere does proletarian democracy better flourish, or the will of the people more resolutely express itself. This can be seen in the fact that very often one popular candidate, deeply desired by the people, may stand for all three parties. This compares very famously with so-called democratical conditions in the West.

Today Slaka truly contributes to the great treasure-store of experience accumulated in the construction of socialism. The governmenting body, representing the sovereign will of the worker-people, is the *National Assemblage of the Fatherland*, responsible for policies of revolutionary socialistic emulation, and the advancement of the progress of history. So clear is the will of the people in Slaka that it needs to meet but four days a year. Following always the mott, 'Prolo Solido' ('Solidarity with

18

Slakan shepherd urges into the future his flock

the Workers'), this Assemblage holds representatives of all groups: the committee for State Security, the counsel of Ministers, our military leaders, and even elected representatives. These give their advises to the *Supreme Counsel* ('Politburo') which decides on executions. The Members of the National Assemblage appoint the Politburo, which appoints the President, who appoints the members of the National Assemblage. This insures coherent polices.

Nor does our democracy stop here. In every district and throughout every workerplace or rural collective are the representative devisions of the communistical and anti-fascist parties, and even the young can enjoy by being admitted if their critical thinking is correct to the Young Communistical League. Other associations are the Slakan Hikers' Union and the Union of Slakan Motorists. This structure produces ultimate democratization, and the hopeful sensations so typical of our progressive people's republic.

SLAKA: HOW NOW?

Modern Slaka is a society in the front van of progress. Since the heroic liberation of 1944, about 2 million dwellings of the workers have been constructed, and the average space permitted our livers is 10^2 meters. Notable cities of workers have been built by miracles of prefabrication in Hiririsi'stat and Engel'stat, constituting a tortuous complex of 60,000 pops. The trade unions direct socialistic emulation and are responsible for the sucess of the 'rationalization' movement. Under our fourth Five Year Plan petro-chemical growths nearly doubled almost, and our shoe production multiplied five-folds, producing more than 750,000 units, or three shoes for each of our citizens. Agriculture has more than matched our industrializing development. Over 300 state cooperatives of 1000 ha flourish, and our sour milk and yoghurt production is the envy of the wide world. The advanced watercress industry is a miracle of aggro-organization. Our nuclear technology is proud of its piles, and our RMBK Kiev-type reactor, with its spectacular emissions, offers the means of electrifying our entire people. We wish one day to export these enervating facilities worldwide.

In social welfare and education large expanses have been made. Now our women are gladly paid a wage to make children, and free teachings in Marxist-Leninist arts and sciences are availed from kindergarden to universitet. Our literacies advance by leap and bound, and our sporting achievements are spectacular. Our Olympical synchro-swimmers take many golds, and our hero ballroom-dancers triumph universally in competitional events. Slaka is famous also for its pretty stamps, beloved of filatelists everywhere. In times when in the west economical decline is profuse and unemployment widespreads, Slaka boasts its achievement of total employment for all, along with technical progress. Who cannot envy it? Can you truly say your society is better?? Truly we say modern Slaka is a young nation proudly on the march, its eyes firmly fixed not on the day after yesterday but the day before tomorrow!!!

THE LANGUAGES OF SLAKA

by Katya Princip
(People's Novelist)

For me, as a good writer, what an unusual honour it is to be asked to write in this official state guidebook about the language of my country. Naturally it is an invitation one cannot refuse. So I try to explain you if I can.

Slaka is not a very famous country, and we speak a little language not many understand, not even us. Sometimes it is said that this is because of all the Eastern Europe tongs ours is hardest to learn. It is the purport of this excellent little book – which is fine phrasebook and vocabulary book as well as guidebook – to learn you at once this is not true. Really, I can tell you: to learn our official Slakan language is a matter of simplicity itself. In our country there is a saying (ours is a country full of sayings, and, as we say, 'With so many sayings who needs any doings?'). It tells: 'Of course our language is easy! See, even our babies can learn it!' And of course it is clear that if babies can learn it, so can you. It also helps if you have some Finnish and perhaps a little Hittite. Of course our grammas are different; but if you think our grammas a little odd, think how your English grammas appear to us! All you must remember is that, like Turkish and some others, our language *agglutinates*. This means we make up our cases by adding some more syllabubs. That is not so hard, is it? Really, I think after a few days in Slaka, you will soon be agglutinating too!

Some people like to say that to learn Slaka is a wasting of time, because it is not a world-langauage. About this we also have a saying: 'We are not yet, but we will be.' What I like to tell you is that for your small efforts there come very great

21

rewards. After a week or so of praxis, think, you may be able to read many more official books, just like this one! A bit more endevors, and you will be able to listen to and try to understand the great speechs of our leaders! A little more work yet, and all the great tresors of Slakan literatur will ope to you! You will be able to delight in the great works of all my collegues in the Writers' Union of Slaka, where we all agree that their novels, depicting with such a profound insight the lifes of tractor-drivers as desperately they seek to outdo all previous records of production, are quite definitely major contributions to world-literature! Please, we are not just a little flyshit on the map of the world! So do not think there is a better way to spend your time!

All that makes our language seem difficult to learn is that it is not just one language, but several – and we keep changing them all the time! So in our country no two people speech quite the same, but this is quite natural. It displays you our liberalism, and the historical confusons of our people, who are so mixed up in heritags and so mingled in roots they do not know at all where they stand. Naturally, each region likes to speech in its own way, and every district likes to keep its own dialetics. As a result we have perhaps three main languages, and fiften dialetics, and so of course we do not understand ourselves very well. But do not dismay. With socialistik rationalizations this great 'Tower of Babble' problema has been triumphantly undercome. With characteristikal brilliancy, our wise leaders and party-cadres in their fine offices have given us a new language, Official Slakan, called 'Tom'Slakam', which means, of course, Book-Slakan. They have employed only the best and more perfect fetures of all our languages, and no bad ingredients are used. Thank to this intervention, we are all able to talk to ourselves. Today it is forbidden to write any state pronciament or publish any book in other than 'Tom'Slakam'. Only one problema remains – nobody ever speaks it, so nobody understands it. But then we remember our great saying: 'You cannot build socialism in a day, or produce a baby in a week!' How fortunate we are in Slaka, to have such brave officials who determine to try!

You are confused? Please do not be. Strange to say, an excellent explication of our language is to be found (of all places!!) in a novellum written by a British liberal-burgerish writer M. Bradburyim, called *Rates of Exchange* (in the Slakan translation it is called *Cursi'Cursii*, but this is really quite hard to get). This account of certain so-called going-ons in our country misrepresents from the standspoint of some ignoramus British language-expert the historical realities of Slakan life. However, the reported intervention of national-hero-translator Comrade M. Lubijova puts clearly to this man of strange linguistic pratfalls the basical simplitude of our Slakan tongues:

> It is not so complicate. All you must know is the nouns end in 'i', or sometimes two or three, but with many exceptions. We have one spoken language and one book language. Really there are only three cases, but sometimes seven. Mostly it is inflected, but sometimes not. It is different from country to town, also from region to region, because of our confused history. Vocabulary is a little bit Latin, a little bit German, a little bit Finn. So really it is quite simple. I think you will speak it very well, soon.

This description makes clear that the task is straightforward, though we do not to this day know whether that British visitor succeeded it.

However apart from such passages the novellum of Bradburyim is not to be commended. It is not a useful story, and alludes to events that did not happen, particularly a language revolution, the so-called 'Revolution of the UUU's', when liberal elements sought to change the language. And though nothing that book did describe did ever take place, we are proud to say that these events which did not occur afford decisive proof that free and frank discussion, dissent and criticism are always permitted in my country.

Why, if these events did not occur, is it necessary (or even wise) to mention it? Here you must know another of our sayings: 'It is best not to forget the past entirely; you will probably need it again in the future.' We also like to say: 'A good Slakan knows two languages, this for now, the other for later.' The fact that this or that has not happened in the past does not deny that it may happen in the future. Here, in a very fraternist spirit, I like to offer a small word of advise. If you come to my country, and you wish to open your mouth, be just a little cautious. If you arrive in a time of linguistic uphevals – and I think you will know this by the sound of gunfire in the streets, for we take our languages quite seriously – take a care: keep down the head, and mind also your 'i's' and 'u's'. In these days it is best to speak only 'Nova'Slakam'. In other days it is not. As we like to say: 'History is a fickle mother, and sometimes she is bad father as well.' Really, it is best to get this right unless you like to stay in my country a very long time, and perhaps you do not.

But such confusions should not muddle you so much. Our country is delightful, and you will find that quite a lot of young people here speak some Englisch, especially the words of Punk Floyd songs. This phrasebook you hold will do all that is necessary, and presents you all familiar useages and probable situations. This will help you to find the Cathedral, or the lavatory, to make friends in street or in the sleazed ambiance of some gipsy art-strip club, and communicate well with our friendly police and national security force if you are detained

---

Interpretational Facilitations

Interpretors of the most expert kind are always availed in Slaka, for, congresses, diplomatical purports, commercialistic enterprises, etc. Apply only to the Burosk Dolmetschim, Min'stratii Kulturi Komit'etiii, and your incomprehensible problems will be over!!!

for currency or other severe offenses against the state. Therefore we advise you to carry this book with you at all times. Perhaps it is also a guidebook to your own country. Here we have another saying: 'Always read a book twice, once on the pages, once between the pages.' A good book has many uses, so carry it carefully, read it often, look in it everywhere. And, whatever you do, this time do not lose it!!

GETTING AROUND IN SLAKA: A HANDY PHRASEBOOK AND GUIDE

CONTENTI

MAKING A TOUR IN SLAKA

SLAKA: WHY TO COME?

So much for our backgrounds, but let nothing detter your visit to this beautiful place. Truly Slaka is a country not to be missed. Large woods invite sportsmen, and 'vacations in saddel' delight horse-riding fans. Especially lovely is the month of May, when the magnolias bloomb. But other excellent seasons include autum, spring, summer, and winter. However you like to come in Slaka, we oblige. And if our transports or hotels are sometimes not quite perfect (we do not mind to make a criticicm), we recall a wise saying of our Russian brothers: 'A little rigour makes a holiday better!'

Slaka has always been famous to travelers, a land for all of curious tastes. Our own great traveller, Vrop Personip, who stems from Gilt, a town famous for its humours, was asked once 'Why come to Slaka?' He thought for many minutes, then retarted: 'Everywhere you go in Slaka there is something, and then a lot more!' If asked what more there was, he thought for minutes, then repiled: 'I do not know, but you will find it!' His wise saw is long-remembered with us. Truly in Slaka travellers have found always that 'lot more'!

So we invite you!!! attend to our cities and townlets, our congress and our festivis!!! We invite you!!! come, rest at our spars and drink the water in our baths!!! We invite you!!! dance at our gipsy nightspots, or sip our hot meads and salt almons in our tavernas, or sit under a bird-filled tree and enjoy a village wed!!! We invite you!!! join please our gourmandizings, enjoying our famous speciality 'sarkii banati' (folded pate on a bun)

28

or the great delicatesse of the Pritprip region 'tortosa bakum' (tortoise baked in its shells). We invite you!!! drink with us in our vinous regions, and remember in their native sets even the strangest potions acquire a delirious taste! We invite you!!! to our prehistorical deposits, our centres of balneation, our busting marketplaces!!! We invite you! Do you come?

You will not regret. For holiday-making there are fine modern hotels, where your room will often have balcony with WC. For the sun-loafer, there are our fine beeches. For the glutton, Slaka is a lasting festival of oat cuisine. The dionysian disciple cannot fail to become delirious with our fine local vintages. The hiker will delight in our famous long marches, and the mountain-climer will not forget our faces. Folklore lovers will delight in our yogurt competitions, where dances by pheasants in their long skirts are frequently performed, accompanied by their women on the bagpipes. The archeological digger will enjoy many a poke in our ruins. Theater-lovers will delight in the products of our great 'Gorky-Ensemble' Theatre Company, and do not forget the Puppet Theatre, next to the Russian Embassy, which gives great delight to small audiences. The music-buffer will make by instinct for the great 'Z. Leblat Musiology Festivi', and leave with our filharmonias still ringing in his ears. If of operatic bent, you will undoubtedly seek out our great 'Oper Z. Leblatim' oper-hus, where you may see a major operatic repertoire with the world's leading singers mounted by our great operturge Leo Fenycx (geb. Praha, 1958).

Truely, in Slaka there is something for all!!!

SLAKA: WHEN TO COME?
Always famed for its wethers, Slaka offers you delight at all seasons of the year. Springs in Slaka, celebrate in song and story, are a balmy time, when warm zephyrs of the mediterranean meet wafts of the North to create a climat always melba and never extreme. Summer delights us, and when our fine sun brills it is the Slakan way to retire to our lakesidings and make one endless

sportfest. Autumn when the sun is gentile is our fruitiest time, when we suck mouthwatered appels and collect the grapes and olives from which we make our exceptionalist wines. Winter with its snows and fogs is ski-time, when we like to slip on our slopes and then all foregather to make our famous hot baths in the woodshed. Neither hot neither cod, Slaka is through the year long a place of unstinting resort. Come when you like, you find wether to please. When to come in Slaka? Any time!!!

For seasonal coutume we offer this advise. Almost never does it rain in Slaka, but raincloths are desirable in some season, mostly spring, summer and autumn. For traditional reasons many of our people carry umbrellas in the streets, so take good care of them!!! In summer bring sporting gears, from the whites of tennis to the latexes of skindivering. In winter we recommend a furpiece and perhaps it is wise to wear a rubber on your foot.

SLAKA: HOW TO COME?

By Airs
The state airline, Comflug, tries to fly to all countries with which Slaka has friendly relations. In a mere 4 hours from London (usually longer from New York), their weekly flight will wisk you to a new vacation wonderland. The airport at Slaka, 'Flyt'dromo Z. Leblatim', is but 5km/8mi from the city. Busses to the central Comflug office, Wodji'mutu 217 (no chekkin facilities), depart by the hour. Tickets must be bought in avance at the airport tobacco stall (Littii) and are not available in board. Only the orange-coloured taxis should be used.

By Seas
You cannot come by seas to Slaka.

By Rails
No direct train-routes like to come from the West of Europe to Slaka. Yet indirect trains from such centres as Riga or Bucharest

bring many travellers. Such trains stop at many places, and sometimes at stations, in our country. Train service inside Slaka is of two kinds: quite fast (es'pressii) and quite not so fast (rapidii). There are two classes (III and IV) and IIIrd class is commended to travellers who like their comforts and prefer to be seated. Some *es'pressi* bear on occasion a dining car, though often reserved for party officials. (Attenzie: photygrafing of trains and transportation systems is a state crime, suspected to severe penalties.)

By Roads

No main autoroutes pass through our country, because we like to keep it nice, but British travellers will be accustomed to this. But Slaka lies not remotely from the route Berlin-Calcutta and Moscova-Sevilla. Slakan roads are often asphlat and many are free of boulders. Foreign drivers are permitted an entry at 3 frontiers, Pilaf, Splat and Vitosk. Insurances and permits of travel may be purchased (75 vloskan) from the boarder. There are more than 15 stations of petrol (bin'zinii) in the country, and tourists may buy with western currency at special high prices. Types of petrol: regular (regli), 15 octane, and extra (ex'trii), 18 octane. We practise our driving on the right, but pass only on the inside. Traffic regulations are a little distinctive: e.g. forbidden is to overtake haycart. Also forbidden is to drive at night, drunk, and in a restricted area, especially at once. Speed limit: town, five vlods an hour, countries, eight vlods an hour. Everywhere there are special police patrols to help you and tow you somewhere. Parts of western cars are not availed,

---

Distances in Slaka

The main unities of long measurement in Slaka are the nippii and the vlod (73½ nippin = 1 vlod). For convenience, one vlod = 10 kilometers or 2 miles (approximative).

---

but our mechanicals are very resourceful. However you do well to travel with screwdriver and string. Penalties for accident are severe, and our peasants know this and sometimes like to have them. And remember!!! in our country we like to drive with a little excitement, so expect always on the road some surprises!!!

Getting Around in Slakan: A Phrase Book

Often Slakan is considered one of the more difficult European languages. Here we show you it is not true!! This small phrase-book is designated to help, presenting probable situations and familiar usages. Remember, we like to write our language with both the Cyrillic and Roman alfabets, but most of our semiotics are in both.

Also included is a list of vocabulary. One look and you will see how very simple our language is!!!

AT THE AIRPORT
[Remember!!! Our Slakan state airline, Comflug, likes to fly to most capitals with which our country has a friendly relation!!!]

This is the airport	Hic fo flyt'dromo
There is the entrance/exit	Hac fo invat/otvat
Go to arrivals/departures	Invo in'venii/ot'venii
Have a wonderful trip!!	Bone vy'aggii!!
Please check your baggage	Chekkii'chekkii, da?
What is your destination?	Quo toc destino?
You want to leave our country?	Toc volo parto no statiim?
The plane is full	Flytbom fo pleto
There is another in three days	Ultro in trezim diazim
But that is full too	Ma hoc fo pleto als
Do not be dejected	Nei winj'o
We have found you a place	No trovo plaz'scim

Someone has been taken off the plane	No grabo oi dan flytbomum
The passengers are boarding	Vy'aggii fendo inburdi
Follow the signs	Suvo semioticii
Slakan Nationals/Foreign Nationals	In'diginii/ot'diginii
Passengers/Groundstaff	Vy'agii/Terri'towii
Flightcrew/Cabincrew	Flugsi'mannnii/flugsi'frolikii
Identity check/Currency check	Ident'ayii/Geld'ayii
X-ray check/Body-search	Skelli'makii/Bot'proddii
Be so good as to undress	Nakiii!
Kindly bend over	Bend'ii!
This is forbidden	Hic fo prohibito
That is indecent	Hac fo porno
Those cannot be exported	Ho nei poso ex'porto
Have a good flight!!	Bone flugso!

ON THE PLANE

Welcome aboard	Velki in'burdu
Fasten your seat-belts	Lupi lupi
No smoking	Noki roki
Do not take photographs	Noki fyto'gryfi
Pay attention	Attenzie
Read your leaflets	Voyo sifti'pimflitim
Lifebelts are under the seats	Flatt'in umper stuli
Oxygen masks will appear	Maskaya ick'sgeni flipifloppa
Here are the emergency exits	Poddo immerg'nicina
The crew have parachutes	Flugsimanni ho puffi'packim
The stewardesses do not serve drinks	Flugsi'froliki nei ho buvam
The toilets are closed	Evak'ebo fermo
Small delays may occur	Flyto di'verto
We have found a good place	No trovvo plazscii possibli
You will like it here	Toc amico
Now we are landing	Standaki noc
Stay in your seats	Resti in stuli

The police will inspect you	Mulit'zayuu toc voyo
The soldiers will protect you	Soldati toc tecto
Do not move	Noki moti
Do not speak	Noki sondo
The bus will take you	Auto toc fendo
Push to the back	Shuvo bakom
It is only four hours	Solo versi ora
Welcome to Slaka!	Velki in Slakam!!

Clocks

Slakan time is 2½ hours in front Greenwitch Meal Time, except in provincial cities and the countryside, where local custom prevails.

SLAKA: AT THE FRONTIERS

Visa

All visitor require a passport with visa, obtenu at the 'Consolii dan Popliim Prol'etaniim Stattim Slakam' in most Western capitals. Seventeen copies of photographs are require. On arrive, visitors must registrate with the local Militia each night and change residences only with permissions. Passipotti are normally returned in a few hours, unless there is a little confusion.

Customs

Our customs like to be very friendly, but certain rules are strict. Is forbidden to bring to Slaka: a) fusils and boms, b) benzines and acids, c) drugs and hihis, d) books and papers, c) pornos and vidi'nasties. Dutyfree is foods, drinks and tabacs needed in holiday, but all personals must be delared and listed on entry. Gifts of a value of 100 vloskan may be taken at depart, but only if on our 'exportable list', and not on our new 'unexportable list' which arrests the exports of our national tresors.

Currence (Geld'ayii)

Is forbidden to enter or leave Slaka with Slakan monies. Also restricted is the money brought into the country. Each traveller makes a declaration emptying the pockets and undertaking to change so much a day. Change may be performed only at the offices of the state bank (Burs'ii Prole'tanii) or at the change-desk (camb'ayii) of your Cosmoplot hotel. All currencies must be accounted at departure, so keep always your recipes.

The units of currence are the vloska and the bitti (one

hundred bittiin to the vloska). As a rough guide, one bitti purchase matchbox, five a postcard. With one vloska you may take twenty times the tram, or buy 2 kilo tomates, or 1 kilo dry sausage. With fifty vloskan, maybe you like a nice trouser, or a beautiful lady. There are four rates of exchange: diplomatic rate, congress rate, business rate and tourist rate. All rates fluctate according to the decline of the western economy. (Attenzie: illegal transactions are sometimes offer. Remember, we say in friendly way!!! Currence offences are severe crimes against the state, and attract the most severe penaltos!!!)

MEETING, GREETING, ETC.

This is a meeting	Hic fo receptii
Here is a greeting	Hac fo grussi
How are you?	Com'fo, da?
Very well	Bone, da
I am delighted to be here	Mi boyo fendo in Slakam
We are delighted to have you	No fo boyo als
I bring greetings from our comrades	Mi grusso dan cam'radakam
I bring love from our government	Mi grusso dan burosk'nikki
Are you my interpreter?	Toc fo mi dolmetschi?
Do you speak Slakan?	Toc ho lingam Slakam?
I am a foreigner	Mi fo estrangi
I have not been here before	Nei fo vanti in Slakam
I do not speak the language	Nei parlo lingam Slakam
I cannot understand you	Nei capisco
Don't you speak English?	Nei parlo lingam Anglistikam?
We speak it a little	No ho poco
But not much	Ma na mamoro
You speak too quickly	Toc lungo malto volto
Please talk more slowly	Lungo lenti
More slowly still	Lenti ma
Write it down	Scripto, da?

36

We can't read it	No nei terpo
This is very difficult	Hac fo malto stupido
Please don't leave me	Nei lasco
Help, help	Sosso!! Sosso!!

FINDING DIRECTIONS

Can someone help me?	Poso sosso?
I am a friend	Mi fo amicato
Pleased to meet you	Favi grusso
How can I assist you?	Com'sisto?
Where is the tramstop?	Quo trovo halti'truggiim?
Or else the bus-stop?	Als halti'autobussom?
I wish to go to the city	Volo fendo in stattim
I have much baggage	Malto baggii
There is no problem	Nei problema
What are you doing?	Qua fo?
Where are you going?	Qui fendo?
He has taken my baggage	Ig tako mim baggim
Make way	Accesso, pardi
Sorry, excuse me	Pardi
Follow that man	Suvo hac frollin
He has disappeared	Ig parito
This is an emergency	Hac fo immerg'nicina
Do not worry	Nei frenzo
Here we do not steal	Nei grabo hac
It is a crime against the state	Multo penalto
There is a policeman	Voyo, jend'armi
He takes you to the policehouse	Toc fendo in jend'arm'nosk
You must make a statement	Toc fo splicaro
And stay there three days	Oc resto trezi diazi
I do not want my baggage	Nei volo mim baggiim
It was very old	Malto antish'ki
Thanks for your help	Malto slibob po sosso
I hope to see you again	Spiro nac toc voyo
I hope you see me again	Spiro nac mi voyo
You have helped me very much	Toc fo malto soso

I don't know what I would   Nei capisco quo fo sin toc
    have done without you

TRAVELLING TO THE CITY

Can I get a taxi here?   Mi grabo tacksi, hic?
I have waited an hour   Mi stando una ora
Is this an official taxi?   Tacksi officiale?
Take me to the city centre   Tako mi in centrim, da?
You drive very fast   To chargo masti, da?
Please drive more slowly   Lenti, lenti, nei?
More slowly still   Malto lenti, da
He was only a peasant   Agrico solo
His friends will assist him   Amici sisto
Please turn down the music   Devolvo musika, da?
Much as I admire military   Toc concerto milut'aristiku fu
    bands   superbo
What a lovely view!   Qua voyo dur'agayo!!
The countryside is splendid   Rurim fo splendido!
And what a fine city!   Qua stattii boyo!!
Here are the workers'   Voyo, hi'risi proletan'ayii
    apartments
They are a miracle of   Miraculo structi, da?
    construction
This is an industrial district   Hic fo plaz'scii meckanistici
See the records of production   Voyo semiotica product'im
Our workers work long hours   Proli labore oram mamoram
They do not get tired   Nei fo flaggo
That is why we are successful   Hac tecto no fama
Work is good   Laboro fo bone
But everything is closed on   Fermi samzi, naturo
    Saturday
What is this fine place?   Quac fo hac structi grandi?
This is your hotel   Voyo, toc otelli
I have enjoyed our trip   Bone tui, slibob
What is the fare!   Koliko po vy'aggiim?
For you, a special rate   Po toc, cursi specialistiki

38

Better than the clock	Melio quan tictok
Please pay in dollars	Dollari, nei?
Alas, I have no change	Nemi camb'ayii, pardi
Thanks, guv	Malto slibob, cam'radaki
I hope you can manage	Toc fendo okay, okay?
I have a bad back	Vertibri fibli

Telephones and Posts

Slaka has telefonic communications with many parts of the world. To make an international call you must book one day in advance with your hotel telefonist or the police. To keep tidy streets, telefon booths do not litter our cities, but post offices have faculties for interior calls. Telephone numbers may be obtained from the Ministry of State Security or the communications officer in your hotel. If you here strange noises in the line, remember!!! our system is different!

Letters and postcards may be sent abroad by delivering them personally to the People's Post Office.

TRAVELLING IN SLAKA

COSMOPLOT WELCOMES YOU!!!

The word of welcome in Slakan is 'velki', except sometimes 'grussi', and always we like to say 'velki in Slakam'. Tourism in Slaka is a well-practised art, with every convenience. For under the wise dirigation of our Ministry of Tourism all tourist enterprises have been designated to the state tourist board, 'Cosmoplot'. Famous for their organizations and working beneath their proud slogo 'We have ways of making you tour!', Cosmoplot operates all tourists hotels and trippings, plans your congress and overseas your vacance from starts to finishes. Their desks are in the airporto and the lobbys of all hotels, and their fine hostesses in distinctive blue uniforms delight in instructing and telling you to have a very good holiday!!

Today most travellers like to go inside packages, and 'Cosmoplot' affords tours of every kind from the historical to the mercenary. But even if you do not fit in a package, you may still avail of 'Cosmoplot's' incomparable services. Trained personal will put you in a room, make sure you trip when you want to, and in general ensure your pleasurable experiences. They will provide you with girl guides, and try to interpret you in any way. Only ask – it is their work and they love to service you. In fact really it is impossible to tour in Slaka without their facilitations!!!

YOU LIKE AN HOTEL???

For the benefit of tourists who like a place to stay, Cosmoplot provides hotels in many of our cities and countrysides. Here to

Prospect of artisan dwellings with twin towers of HOGPo

highest standards are availed all the facilities of western comforts. Do you like a room that has bad-wc? It is available for all-in prices. Free services include the transport of baggages inside the chamber, cloth's brushes, footwipers, information of the temperature of the air. Only small charges are made for a wash and an iron. All foreign guests must stay in these places. This is to avail them of further advantages, for all have automatically insurance against death, loss of power to work due to accident, and disappearance of baggages. Lobbies often contain a tobacco shop, a perukist, and a Wicwok foreign currency shop for the delight of the turstii. Here with your fingertips you may buy magazines and sweets, postcards and matches, some decorated, vestments of leather and carpet, folkloric tissues, our fine party newspaper, *P'rtyii Popu'latiii*, the English *Morning Star*, and the best Slakan novels and poems in fine British translattions. Here, if you do not have it, you may buy this very book!!! Also conveniently place is a desk for exchange. Remember to use it!!! Foreign visitors must change so much a day. We make this rule

41

only to facilitate your opportunities of shopping, enabling you to purchase our excellent export products (the notable bottled beetroot!! the incomparable brown shoes!!) and enjoy the privileged arrangements in hotel, restaurant and art-strip club.

Every major town affords these magnificent hotel-palaces. In Slaka leading hotels are «Hotel Cosmoplot-Slaka»*** «Hotel Cosmoplot-Orbis»**, «Hotel Cosmoplot-Volga»**, and «Hotel Cosmoplot-Yalta»†. All afford complet services of eating, drinking and sleeping. For example, in «Hotel Slaka», do not neglect to visit: ***RESTAURANT SLAKA: offered are such delicacies as, Kyrbi Churba (mutton soap), Cotelette de l'Amateur (chop-lovers' chops), Sarkii Banatu (folded pate) and the notable Boyard Plate, animated with folkloric singeres and typical orchester:***NIGHTCLUBZIPZIP: the personal are clothed as peasants from mountains and national fame artists give remarkable performances of, jiggling, songing, art-strip, etc.: ***BARR'II TZIGANA: the personal are in coutumes Romany, and both spiritual and non-alcoolical drinks are availed.

Further afield, in the interior, at mountain or balneological resorts, hotels both traditional and modern welcome your sojourn. At «Hotel Cosmoplot-Kosmos»**, in Glit, a waterwheel perpetually roules, and the ristorant, perched high on rocks, offers a superb vertigo, while sheep are roasted as you watch. A bar in the arabesque style proposes romanticism, and the nearby verdure provides you with a place of quiet resort. At «Hotel Cosmoplot-Siberia»††, in Nogod, a beach is afforded with comfortable bathchair and we invite yo to spend many plesant hours in the lake.

Whatever your taste, from luxury to primitivism, we are happy to provide. Our lakeside resorts offer cabins and right on the spot you may hire a tent or field-kitchen for a camp experience.

No doubt about it, all will be sattisfied by their sojourn in this beautiful land. And know again our other slogo, 'Cosmoplot, tota po toc servic'im ('Cosmoplot is always at your service'). Yes, truly we can say 'Velki in Slakam!!'

REGISTERING AT THE HOTEL

[Hotels in Slaka are run by the state tourist board, Cosmoplot. Their comforts are outstanding and all western currencies are taken.]

Welcome to your Cosmoplot hotel	Velki in toc otellim Cosmoplottim
It has a newspaper stall	Habo litti
A hairdresser, a tourist shop	Py'ruki, Wicwok
A desk to change your money	Camb'ayii
A restaurant, a nightclub	Ristor'anti, Club Zip-Zip
There is a nice bar downstairs	Bone barriii umper
With many lovely ladies	Malto froliki amici
They are forbidden	Stricto prohibito
But we like visitors to be happy	Ma no volo boyo no vy'aggim
First you must register	Primo, fo reg'ystrayo
Here is the registration desk	Hac reg'ystrayii
Just past the man in the big hat	Passo frollin dan krapam mamoram
I want a room	Volo rom
There is no room	Nema rom
Oh, you have Slakan currency	Ah, vloskan!
Perhaps one small room	Solo poco rom
I'll take it	Tako, slibob
Fill the registration form	Scripto permi, da?
Your name, address	Nami, husi
Street, Town, City, Country	Stratti, Osk, Statti, Dig'ini
Name of Father, name of Mother	Nami papi, nami mami
Passport number	Nombo passi'potti
Identity card number	Nombo ident'ayii
Date of birth	Dati nati
Where from? Where to?	Fendo vanti? Fendo nac?
What for? Why here?	Purporti? Rat'yonali?
This is your doorkey	Locki, da?

Your hotel identity card	Identay'ii, da?
No card, no breakfast	Nei hac, nei for'tost
Please carry my bags	Porto baggi, slibob
They are too heavy	Fo mamoro
Is there a porter?	Hac fo baggi'manni?
He is at a meeting	Noki baggi'manni
Where is the maid?	Quo fo sklaf'rom'rub'froliki?
The maid is on holiday	Sklaf'rom'rub'froliki fo festo
Go to the lift, elevator	Fendo in up'zippim
Alas, it does not work	Noki fendo
There is the staircase	Hac fo up'ploddi
Yours is the seventh floor	Toc ho plino septi
Enjoy the facilities of your Cosmoplot hotel!!	Resti bone po otellim Cosmoplottim!!

FINDING YOUR ROOM

Which is the number of my room?	Qua schlaff'roma?
It is down the corridor	Fendo pa kafkam
I will show you	Mi proddo
I am the floor maid	Mi fo du'enna
I sit here always	Mi suto simper
I watch over you all the time	Mi toc toto surveio
This is your bedroom	Hei, toc sklaf'rom
I will unlock it	Mi oppo
Look, a bathroom!	Voyo, badi!
There is no toilet paper	Nema bad'i'papuri
You should bring your own	Obligato porto bad'i'papuri
I like this room very much	Amico malto sklaf'rom
It has been cleaned very well	Netto splendido, ha!
We like to work hard	Amico laboro
We do not accept tips	Noki retro'mannii
We work for the state	Laboro po stattim
But my mother is ill	Ma mati in'bone
My uncle is dying	Nunco fo morti
My child is incurable	Mi petto vasto
Thank you very much	Multo slibob

STAYING IN YOUR HOTEL ROOM

Have a nice stay	Bone resti!!
We are not responsible	Noi pendo on no
Lock your door at all times	Noppo portim simper
Vacate room by nine o'clock	Ora parto, 9:00
Breakfast is available	For'tost, 5:00–7:30
Lunch is regularly served	Mi'tost, 11:20–12:00
There is an excellent dinner service	Bak'tost, 5:00–6:30
Ring for our laundry maids	Sono lavo'frolikim
They love to wash you	Amico toc lavo
For a small fee	Mamoro grato
List your customery	Listo habitom
Declare your underwearings	Scripto umper'habitom
Pants and knickers	Wy'frontii, combii
Vests and braziers	Bodici, floppa'chekki
Shirts and blouses	Blusii, blusi'frolikii
Jackets and trousers	Vesti, pantii
Do not make iron in your room	Nei ferro
Do not fume in your bed	Prohibito!! Noki roki in sklaf'burdim
Take fire precautions	Attenzie!!! Combusto!!!
Listen always for the bell	Attendo clappa'clappa
Immediately leave your belongings	Lasco bagiim pronti
Do not use the lift	Noi fendo up'zippim
Climb out of the window	Parto po fen'strum
We are not responsible	Noi pendo on no
Have a nice stay	Bone resti!!

Electrical faculties

The voltage is 110 AC/DC (20 cycles, 8 watts). Wall-fitments are of the usual five-pin type. Electrical shaving in hotels is an offence against the state, attracting severe penalties.

LEAVING YOUR HOTEL

I had a nice stay	Mi fo bonem restim
The service was splendid	Servico splendido
The food was out of this world	Mamo'tost incred'ibili
Everywhere I was looked after	Mi surveyo tota
Where do I pay my bill?	Qui fo tottii?
There is the cash-desk	Kassa do, da?
Run by the State Bank	Po Burs'ii Prol'anii
Here is your account	Voyo tottii
This is a lot	Hei, mamora!
Your rate of exchange is bad	Cursii mali, da?
The vloska is rising	Vloska levo
The pound and dollar are sinking	Punti oc dollari lapso
Due to the degeneration of the West	Ecun'moco chil'ial
We have a good economy	Ecun'moco splendido
Founded on socialist principles	Princ'ipo socialistikum
It is far too much	Totti malto malto
I cannot pay it	Nei capo pagayo
You have to pay it	Obligo pagayo
You must have a credit-card	Toc ho kartam'umperi'plastikum?
You are a westerner	Toc fo occidento
We always can fix things	Experto rematiko
We have been traders for centuries	No fixo po millen'ariim
Just sign here	Scripto, da?
Oh, your telephone call to Japan	Hei, telefono in Nippom
And you burned the eiderdown	Als singo duvetim
That is very serious	Maximo penalto
I forgot to include them	Oblivo, oblivo
But your bank will settle	Bursii solvo
Please come again	Reveni, da?
Cosmoplot is always at your service	Cosmoplot, tota po toc servic'im

YOU LIKE TO MAKE A SHOP???

In our country we have a saying (always a saying!): 'Put a Slakan on an island and he starts a shop!' This alludes to the tradition of trade which has always been so much a piece of the Slakan caracter. Because of its place at the international cross-road, the goods and chatells of all lands have usually found their ways to Slaka. In our gay street markets peedlers like to peedle vegetables of infinite strangeness, and shops of distinction carry imitations of major branded goods. If you like to buy a 'Pirker' pen, a 'Guchi' shoe, or a 'Famous Mouse' scotch, you will probably find that somewherre in Slaka.

Where to go? Walk first to the great shopping bulevar 'Stalingradsi'mutu', where specialty and delicacy shops of each kind abound. Do you like to filatalize? Do you want a glass boot? In elegant windowdress you will doubtless find. Go to the bespoke men's shop and suit yourself!! Go to the elegant woman's boutique and try the lingueries!! And then there are the distinctive Slakan comodes: glasswear, fine brod-eries, carved wooden things of the foret. Our peasants when they do not labour at their field love to take up the knife at home, while, perhaps, the wife of the house cardles and spinds.

Eminent on Stalingradsi'mutu is our great state department story, MUG, so famous that many visit it not to shop. Here is a true world-emporium at last, a tresor-trove of goodies, leder and pelt, woovens and spuns, nitware, bottied beetroot, and 'national cotume' dollies!! Rations of goods come in frequently, and then what a fight to by!!! Trickets and knackknicks of all kinds make fine presence to take home to someone you love or your wife. Only remember!!! certain goods of the 'national tresor' class may not be exported, and can be taken back from you at our friendly customs!!! But this is the luck of the drawer.

Also notice the special foreign currency shop, Wicwok, where are availed: scitches and gins, jeannies 'Levi-Strass' and 'Gloriana Vanderbuilt', barbers 'Filishave', and the likes, at laughable prices. Truly we may remember another Slakan proverb: 'No one leaves Slaka with an empty hand or a full purse!!'

FINDING THE SHOPS

Good morning, today I want to shop	Grussi, mi volo apporto hodi
Fine idea, here our shops are excellent	Bone, no mag'osk fo superbo
Are they expensive?	Fo ex'torto, hei?
No, they are very cheap	Nei, fo in'torto
What are the best things to buy?	Qua apporto bone?
Here everything is superb	Hic tota fo marveloso
We have the best goods from all lands	No habo tingo superbo dan tota mundo
Our people were always traders	No pupli simper fo fixi'fixii
Allow me to show you	Permetto mi proddo
We go to the best shopping street	No fendo po chamsi'lissii
I know you will be tempted	Cognosco toc fo tempto
But don't you need to do something first?	Ma nei habo obligo primo?
I think you like to go to the bank	Flecto toc fendo in bursliim, da?

GOING TO THE BANK

Welcome to the state bank	Grussi in Bursiim Prolet'anim
How can we help you?	Como sisto, cam'radakii?
May I change a little money?	Volo curso geld'ayiim
I should like to go shopping	Mi volo porto
That is our very function	Hac fo exactom purportim
What currency do you have?	Qua geld'ayii?
My money is English pounds	Mi porto puntam Anglistikam
What a pity, the rate is bad	Ah, morti, curso fo male

48

Owing to Japanese competition	Falta Nippon
Kindly tell me the rate of exchange	Dico, qua cursi'cursii?
There are many rates of exchange	Malto cursi'cursii
The diplomatic rate	Cursii diplomatiki
The business rate	Cursii commerkii
The congress rate	Cursii congressii
The tourist rate	Cursii turstii
Yours is the worst	Toc ho malto male
I will just change five pounds	Chango solo funvism puntim
Alas, you must change more	Morte, obligo chango malto
This is our rule	Hac fo no principii
This is to allow you the pleasure of our shops	Po permetto toc apporto malto
I will change you fifty	Mi chango michenti
Then you can have a nice shop	Toc habo porto splendido

THE FOREIGNERS' SHOP

Here is a good place	Hac plazscii boni
Look how full of things it is	Voyo, malto proditti
All the things you are used to	Tota famil'ali
Scotch whisky, London gin	Scitch'viski, Beefeatim
Jeans, videos, stereos	Levii, vivi'nastii, Sonii
All of outstanding quality	Mako excillintii!
Truly it is a cave of Aladdin	Vero cavi Ala'dinii
Of course you must pay in dollars	Solo dollari, da?
This is our famous shop WICWOK	Hac WICWOK
It is for foreigners only	Po strangim, solo
Oh, mind the man in the big hat	Ah, gardo frollin dan krapam mamorem
Try not to offend him	Nei fendo, hei?
It is also for the party officials	Als po parti'cheffii da?

49

THE DEPARTMENT STORE

We will do better in here	No fo ma bone hac
You know this famous place?	Cognosco hic plazsciim notabiliim?
See how big it is?	Voyo qua mamoro
How beautiful it looks?	Qua dur'agayii?
It must be the great department store, MUG	Vero, MUG
You are right	Correcto
How enormous it is!	Malto mamoro!
A true palace of commerce	Pil'azzi commerciii
And filled with such rare things!!	Proditto excillenti!
Glassware, leatherware	Glassii, ledii
Kitchenware, Tupperware	Utin'slii, plastikii
Radios and televisions	Radii, ti'vii
Corkscrews and tin-openers	Pullii, cuttii
All made by state enterprise	Macho priso stattiim!
Do you like to buy a present for your lovely lady?	Volo porto dono po toc frolikin
Perhaps one for your wife as well?	Als po toc femmo?
I see you like underwear	Voyo toc amico umper'habitom
This one, for the deep winter?	Ha, po hiberna
This one, for the hot summer?	Ha, po sveltro
Yes, you have chosen well	Da, toc selecto bone
Now I take you somewhere else	Noc, fendo als

AT THE GROCER/GREENGROCER

What is this fine shop?	Qua fo hac mag'osk raro?
It is our state supermarket PLUC	No super'mag'osk PLUC
Do you see a queue?	Voyo filo?
Only many happy people	Solo malto puplii boyo
Your Western press misleads you	Press imperial'istiki decepto

How much they have to sell!!	Qui produtto mamoro!!
Do you see a shortage?	Voyo minso?
Never have I seen such good things!	Nei voyo si bonem prodittim!
Give me a banana, a carrot	Porto nani, fallii
A beetroot, a melon, a pumpkin	Burschti, lambo, nurdu
What good sugar, give me some	Sugo superbo, mi dono
A thousand grams, two thousand	Milo grambo, duzi milo
There is plenty for everyone	Malto po totam
You have mastered the principles of production	Toc macho principi productim
I will tell all at home	Mi dico mi in'diginim
Everything can be had in Slaka!	Toto trovo in Slakam!!
Try my banana	Tasto nannim, nei?

AT THE CLOTHES SHOP

Now there is a clothes shop	Noc, vesti'mentii
A men's shop, a women's shop	Picca'dillii, froli'kosk
Do you want to look?	Volo voyo?
Yes, they are so fashionable	Da, malto chico
What a nice suit!	Vesto superbo
What is it made of?	Qua pendo?
Good, nylon is my favourite	Bone, amico gluc
And brown is my favourite colour	Oc amico bruno
But do you have my size?	Ma mi shapii?
All sizes are in stock	Tota shapii
May I try it on?	Permetto porto?
What an excellent fit	Shapii exactii!
Is it also a hat-shop?	Krapa'husi als?
A hat to go with this incredible suit	Krapa po vestim superbim
I love this plastic cap	Amico krapam plastikum

51

I'll take three	Volo trezi
You will not regret it	Nei hitznazo
It all suits you very well	Aha, qua bone, qua bone
Look please at these shoes	Voyo sulii
We make them in Slaka	Makina in Slakam
There are three sizes	Trezi shapii
All will fit you	Tota exacto

OTHER SHOPS

Are you tired now?	Toc lapso, da?
You have some problem with your feet?	Toc ploddi, ig pango?
No, I want more excellent shops	Na, ancora mag'osk superbo
The butcher, the baker	Besti, baki!
The chemist, the perfumery!	Apoteko, par'fumi!
The book shop, the cake shop!	Toma'husi, pattii!!
The smart shop, the art shop!	Gal'erri, ort'iski!!!
The furniture shop	Noc in fern'ii
I want a cake, a steak	Volo gattii, cuttii
I want a table, a chair, a settee	Volo tablo, toolo, ottomanii
The taste is incredible	Tasti incredibli!
Please help me carry it	Favi, porto, da!
Up a bit your end	Alto, da?
Stop, look, a craft shop	Hei, heimat'nosk
What extraordinary objects	Ojetti strangii!
They are made by hand in the country	Fato po mano in rurim
Our peasants do not like to be idle	Agrico despico fo inoccupato
They work long hours for the state	Laboro oram mamorem po stattiim
This is beautiful	Qui bellii
I have always wanted a well-pole	Desiro longa plumbi'pullim
You have bought very wisely	Toc apporto sago

You look like a king	Semblo mon'archo
You take home excellent things	Apporto prodittim excillintim
I hope the customs do not stop you	Aspiro don'ayii nei halto

Weighs and Mesures

In Slaka the conventional metrical cystern is used, except only that one kilo = 50 grams.

HOW DO SLAKANS LIVE?

SOCIAL HABITS AND CUSTOMS

All countries of the world have their own custom, and Slaka does not make an exception. Naturally we like you to respect our habits and way of doing things, and perhaps then we all understand each other, no?

Various of our ways confuse some western visitors. In the street it is very polite to follow people, and it is a great mark of respect when people comment on your clothes, sometimes offering to buy them, though this is a crime against the state. Our men when walking like often to hold hands, and this has misled some foreign visitors to their intention, sometimes to a comical result. Also remember please, in Slaka we shake the heads for 'yes' and nod the heads for 'no'. Laughable confusions can result of this. At the toilet, the sign for man is someone in a skirts, and for a woman someone in a trousers. This also can produce a ludicral consequence. Notice also that the familiar western word 'hallo' does not mean the same for us. In our language it is the worst obscenity, and if spoken to a stranger will undoubtedly led to fightings.

Consider also that while conscious of their proud socialistikal heritage our people like to go with a certin formalism. We like to shake hands at you on all occasions, and when we make a business we like a tie at the neck and a hat at the hairs. Our people are hospitalistic, and like much to entertain, usually in a public convenience. When conducting an official affair it is polite always to offer a brandy (rot'vittii) and, remember!!!, when we drink we always like to make toast. Naturally we have

Vronopian pipers with bags

abolisted the burgish forms of address, as 'Mr', and it is always polite to address a man or woman as 'cam'radakii!' (comrade). Though we have no old title of rank, the titles of socialistic service are used (so 'Hero-Worker-Scientist Academikian Professor Dr Rom Rum').

Our formalities often make a surprise for western visitors, who amaze when at, e.g., the first night of the oper, they first discover our stylish glitter and dash. Indeed Hollywood starlings do not exceed our firstnighters in fineries, parfumeries and wonders of dècollage. Amazing indeed when these glittering cognoscentis prove no other than our music-loving workers and peasants, who have cast off the rank sweats of labour for a festive night!!!

So, when you come to Slaka, if a lady, carry a cocktail. If you like to be a man, bear a formal suiting of the better kind. And remember!! in Slaka the cloths of jog are worn but for the jog itself, and we do not port them at social functions!!! Another small advise: in case our climats are variable, we keep our buildings warm, on the inside. In restaurant, nightclub or government bureau you should at once divest, and leave cloths (coats, hats, etc.) at the doorway for a ticket. If you hold to this ticket, such clothings are normally turned back to you when leaving.

At our resorts, watershore chics prevail and good beach apparells are proudly worn. But here one more word of advice!!! Please be topless only if a man, and nude never. Decadent western practises are not admired, and always we like to keep in Slaka a certain decence.

Healths

In Slaka no diseases are truly endemical, but we advise a vaccine for smallpocks, choler, and typoon. The waters of our cities are potable usually, but in the country always fry your waters before tippling. Our medical service is free of charge. When necessary, tourists are taken to hospital. Medical cares are advanced and if you have diseases you will find Slaka a paradice. Please remember!!! if you like to extend your stay with illness, advice the nearest post of the people's Militia, unless you like the interference of our controlling organs!!!

YOU LIKE TO EAT AND DRINK???

Slaka is a well-known dreamland to all lovers of the culinary art, and your stay will be delighted by access to our fine gastronomes. Whether you like a tosthouse or a snackbarr, a sausage palace or a folkloric restaurant, a Paris repas or an Oriental kebab, you are like to be satisfied. In many a pleasing ambience, often animated by a typical chanteuse or a band of brigandish tziganes, you may find plates of almost every kind. Perhaps you like a small dark place with dancing and a short sharp show? Or a typical Slakan set-up where Olde Shoppe customes are demonstrated? Do you wish a gulasch, or a tripe soup? Do you relish bull's testicle, or perhap a special grass from under goats on a mountain? Our delightful restorants offer amazing menus, and when ingredients are availed they will serve you to the best of their disabilities.

Also our country is a festival of fine drinks. Famous specialities are our spiritual brandies, especially rot'vittii, made of the mush of a peach, kicrak, made of the squish of a pear, and lub'duss, made of the glub of a plum. Notable wines come of our state vineyards, and beware please of their remarkable potence. In better places the finest western drinks are availed, as ginni'tonikii and scitch'viskii.

Slaka is also famous for its compulsive nightlife. Famous name acts perform in our state art-strip clubs, and police and military choirs sing our rousing national songs. If you have a taste for dancing, sate it here, with a stately mazurk or a dervish wirl, perhaps in the companies of one of the dark-eyed beauties for which we are famous. (In Slaka we do not like our foreign friends, often missing their wives, to be lonely!!!) And beyond the city of Slaka itself is a wonderland of typical and untypical pleasures, of eating, drinking and nighting, enough for a lifetime of holidays!!!

Do not say we do not know how to live in Slaka!!!

FINDING A RESTAURANT

Today I shall try some Slakan delicacies	Noc mi boyo finim Slakam
Your gastronomic tradition is famous	Tok kukki fo notabili
Please give me your advice	Aviso, da?
You are very wise	Toc fo bone
You have many choices here	Mamoro selectii
Everything is available	Toc trova tota
What is your desire?	Qua loco??
A snackbar or a coffee shop?	Tosti, kaf'iffi'tosti??
A café or a restaurant?	Cave, rist'oranti??
Western style or Eastern style?	Kukki occidentii, kukkii orientalii??
No, I think you like something typical	Nei, volo kukki typico!!
Slaka is a gourmet's paradise	Slaka, paradiso po gurmandim
Every region has its speciality	Toc pitsat ho finam
Many are quite unusual	Mamoro rarii
Do you like to eat a brain?	Volo branim?
The veal of a sheep?	Lakuku kamissim?
The milk chords of a goat?	Yurti bletiim?
Our boiled tortoise is world famous	Tortosi grillii fo fama in globam
I will try anything once	Mi risko
Then I recommend the Restaurant Nada	Aviso Rist'oranti Nada

GETTING A TABLE

Good evening, maître	Bone starrii, maestro
May I have a table for two?	Mi volo tablo po duzim
I do not have a reservation	Ni reservo
But there is no one else here	Ma nemi smako
Perhaps this will help find one	Vloskan, da?
Near to the band, please	Proximo bandi, slibob
Nearer, and indoors	Matto proximo, in husam
I love the moaning of gypsies	Amico whingo tziganim

This table will do very well	Hac fo bone
May we have a cloth on it?	Possi tablo coverto?
Is there a chair?	Volo toolo
One with a cushion on?	Toolo paddito?
May we have a knife and a fork?	Volo nuga, firka
A spoon and a glass?	Zupa, vitri
Please light the candle	Flamo chandlim, da?
Evidently this place is very typical	Claro, hac fo typico, da?

ORDERING YOUR MEAL

Please bring me the bill of fare	Listii, da
Do you have it in English	Listii angliski, da?
Then you must explain it to me	Splico, slibob
Here are our splendid offerings	Voyo no smako splendido
Milk, honey, yoghurt	Piim, mesi, yurt
Soup, fish, game	Sopa, svimmi, flug'ti
Cold meat, warm meat, wild meat	Vurstii, besti, vildi
Vegetables and fruit	Rutti, frutti
Ox, lamb, veal	Harg, kammasi, laakuki
Duck, goose, turkey	Crak'aki, boo'si, gobbli
Bread, cake, pudding	Baki, gati, mushi
Here are three native kinds of soup	Trezi sopa ethnico
Soup with a rabbit	Kupush'nic
Soup with red cabbages	Bursht
Soup with feet in	Kurbi churba
Here are five kinds of fish	Funvsi s'vimmi typico
Fish with a sword	Ruspi
Fish with two pencils in its nose	Dentex
Fish with red hands	Canceri
Fish with a bad face	Dogna
Fish with no face at all	Dovri'sol

Here are three regional meat dishes	Trezi besti nativii
Folded pate on a bun	Sarkii banatu
Thighs of wild boar	Lads'latu
Testicles of bull in best vinegar	Natupashu
This is a flaming dessert	Hac vish'nou
We have found the ideal place	No trovo plazsciim exactim
Alas, none of these are available	Morti, nei possi
I bring you the goulasch	Porti gooli

ORDERING A DRINK

The waiter has taken your order?	Toc ho commando?
A drink with your meal?	Buvi, da?
Water, milk, orange juice?	Voday, piim, pumpi?
Beer, wine, spirits?	Olli, pfin, sp'riti?
Peach brandy, pear brandy, plum brandy?	Rot' vitti, kicrak, lub'duss?
Vodka, Scotch whisky?	Vid'ki, Blackii'whitii?
Gin and tonic?	Ginni'toniki?
Brandy and soda?	Bran'sodi?
A bottle of local wine	Flas'ci pfinim ethnicim
Here is an excellent vintage	Hac vinti excillinti
Made by the state vineyard	Mackino po vintom pro'letaniim
Once it belonged to the monks	Forfram kloster
Now it belongs to the people	Noc teno po poplim
It is far too good to export	Nei ex'porto hac
Our people love it too much	Popli amico malto
It has plenty of body	Malto forcii, hei?
That is why the cork flies out	Pardi, toc pango
Your trousers will soon dry	Pantii seco
Afterwards I recommend the peach brandy	Tardo, aviso rot'vitti
It is definitely not to be missed	Vero, toc nei lasco

PAYING THE BILL

Bring me the bill, please	Porto totti, da?
How much?	Koliko?
Really this much?	Vero?
You have eaten a lot	Malto tosti, da?
You have drunk enormously	Malto buvi als
The cloth is extra	Coverto als
The cushion is supplementary	Paddito als
Peach brandy is not cheap	Rot'vitti fo chero
You smiled at the gipsy	Tzig'anna fo malto chero
She played the violin for you	Ig stringo strad'variim
She sat on your knee	Ig sisto in lappim
American Express?	Hei, Ameksi?
That will do very nicely	Hac fo bone!!

YOU MAKE A SIGHTSEE???

Where Italian peoples like to say 'See Niples and Die', we Slakans like to say 'See Slaka and Live!!' Little doubt that sightseering is one of the plesures of vacation, and 'Cosmoplot' attends to this too. Guides with enormous busses delight to take you to our Slaka view-spots: the Storkian Mountains, the advanced glassblowing factory, the collective state farm.

Or do you like to walk by foot? Here is a brief tour you can make in Slaka. Go from your Cosmoplot hotel to 'Plaz'scii P'rtyii', our central square of finest proportions where the people of Slaka like to make their great parades. Here is the 'Tombo I. Grigoric', Grigoric's Tomb, where in a line you may make your respects. See how all our children love him! Exiting hence, you see facing, with red star, Party Headquarters, and next the Ministry of Strange Affairs and the Ministry of State Security, headquarters of our police of state security, HOGPo.

Pass now to the left down a dark narrow street, and you come to a fine Romanesque building, the People's Palace of Culture, where have offices our Writers' Union, our Journalists' Union, our Painters' Union, our Publishers' Union, our

Bohumil the Shy ignites his monumental gun (detail)

Thespians' Union, and of course our Translattors' Union. Next is the publishing house 'V. I. Leninim', publishers of finely printed books (you hold now one!!!). Next the Young People's Palace, formerly the Theological Seminary. Next the People's Artist Z. Leblat House, which contains a musee of old pianos.

Now greenery delights the eye, for here is the Park of Slakan-Soviet Friendship, where pensioners enjoy their well-deserved repose, carefree children play, and enamored couples dream of the hopeful future. Here notice the Monument of the Liberators, carved by our great socialist-realist art-hero sculptor-painter Lev Pric. Enought for a day!!! Please, you have hardly started, but perhaps you are very tired . . .!!!

MAKING A TOUR OF SLAKA

I am a tourist	Mi fo turst'ii
I want to take a walk	Mi volo prom'nado
I wish to enjoy your fine city	Volo boyo statiim dur'agayiim
Here is an excellent route	Voyo, hac ruti fo splendido
Go along Lenin Boulevard	Fendo po Leninski'cursii
Down Stalingrad Street	Po Stalingradsi'mutu
Through the park of friendship with the Russian people	Po Jardini Camradakii Ivanovskii
Past the Karl Marx Institute of Economics	Po Instit'tutii Ecun'moco Karliim Marxim
Is it easy to find?	Facilo, da?
Ah, this lady will take you	Hac froliki toc tako
She is an experienced interpreter	Dolmetschi officiali
She happens to go in that direction	Fortuno, ig fendo po da
She does not cost you a penny	Nei pagayo una bittim!!
What wonderful streets!	Mutu marv'osa!!
What wonderful buildings!	Qua structi nob'lii!!
How well they are restored	Bone restoro
What is this splendid place?	Que, hac structii superbo?
The Ministry of Culture	Min'stratii Kulturi Komit'etiii
The Museum of Old Pianos	Musi tinki'tinki antiski
The Russian Embassy	Embassadi Ivanovski
The State Puppet Theatre	Dram'hus puppetii Prolet'anii
The Z. Leblat House	Husi Z. Leblatim
Here in Z. Leblat Street	Hac Z. Leblatsi'mutu

63

Just off Z. Leblat Square	Po Plazscii Z. Leblatsim
We are proud of Z. Leblat	No miro Z. Leblat
He invented our folkish musicology	Trovo no tradiim musik'im poplim
We give him many prizes	Po ho, malto presco
Alas he is two hundred years dead	Ma ig morto duzicentim anum
Don't you love our city?	Amico no stattim?
I have never seen anywhere better	Nei voyo statiim maltom superbim
Now I show you something special	Hei, toc voyo tankim espec'm

VISITING A STATE MOMUMENT

Just go down this dark passage	Fendo pa kafkam grisim
Stop by the soldiers	Halto po militar'iim
You recognize this man?	Hac frollii, toc cognosci?
I have never seen him before in my life, honestly	Nei voyo forfram, suro
He is Grigoric, our great liberator	Grigoric, no mamoro liberato
He freed us to the Russians	No libero dan Ivanovskiim
That is why we love him	Suro no amico malto
He looks alive but he is dead	Semblo vivo, ma fo morto
That is why we embalmed him	Hac qui no mummo
This is his famous tomb	Hac ig tombo famoso
See how all the children come	Voyo, totti veni
And all our peasants from the country	Als agricii dan fermii collectivii
They bring their flowers	Porto flureskim
Do you do this for your great men?	Toc fo po frollinim mamoremim?
Perhaps you do not love them so much	Poso toc nei amico si immalto
Now we go somewhere else	Na fendo als
Or perhaps you are very tired	Toc lapso, nei?

IN THE PEOPLE'S PARK

This is a park of the people	Jardini prolet'anii, hei?
Future citizens come to play	Totsi jumpo
Pensioners enjoy well-earned repose	Gerat'rici sunno
Our soldiers take a deserved rest	Militarii glaro
How pretty the flowers are	Malto flureski, da?
How well behaved everyone is!	Malto sereno, als!!
Does that man follow you?	Hac frollin toc suvo?
What does he say to you?	Qua dico?
He asks to buy your trousers	Volo apporto toc leggim
Do not listen	Ma nei attendo
That is a crime against the state	Malto penalto
Probably he is a stool pigeon	Suro, provoc'tato
He has gone behind a tree	Disparo po pulim
That is not good	Nei bone, da?
They are very nice trousers	Leggim superbo, nei?
How much do you want for them?	Quanto totto?

VISITING A PUBLIC PLACE

This is our great square	Voyo, Plazscii'P'rtyii!!
Here we have our great demonstrations	Hic fo no man'fustii
Over there the National Assembly	Hac fo Prasidium
Once it was the royal palace	Bakom, pal'itzo monarchico
Now our People's Government meets here	Noc semblo no Apparat'i Prolet'anii
Next door Party Headquarters	Voyo, Burosk P'rtyiim Prolet'aniim
Where work our Party-Chiefs	Qui laboro no P'rti'cheffii
The Ministry of Strange Affairs	Min'stratii Uffufii Estrangiim
The Berlin Wall Café and Pastry Shop	Cave'patii Berlinim

The Slakan Hikers' Union	Co'opo Vandistiim Slakam
There are the civil servants	Malto burosk'nik, da?
See their nice official cars	Voyo Volgam!!
With the lace curtains on the windows	Blindi el'ganti po fenestrim
How well they look after us!	Iggi no gardo malto!!
The Ministry of State Security	Min'stratii Stifufii Stattiim
They inspect all our activities	Ig specto tota no fo'do
To make sure we are happy	Po suro no fendo boyo
Do not go in there!	Prohibito fendo!!
I stopped you just in time!	Mi toc halto bonem tempem!!

AT THE ART GALLERY

This is the gallery of People's Art	Hic fo Galeri'ortiski Proletanii
Our Worker-Artists èxhibit here	Hac man'fusto no malorim ort'hero'im
See the pictures of tractors	Voyo, pittori tract'imim
Really you can almost smell them!	Vero, toc poso skento!!
Our artists love socialist realism	No malori amico realismusim social'iskim
No decadent tendencies have taken root	Prohibito declinim imperial'istim
The work of the great Lev Pric!	Voyo, pittori Levim Pricim!!
How well he can draw a tank!	Vero, bombom superbim!!
Look, a sculpture to our liberators!	Voyo, plintho po libero!!
You must be getting tired	Volo sklaffo, da?

OTHER THINGS TO SEE

I think we have had a very nice tour	Bone turistiki, nei?
But this is enough for today	Suffico, da?
I will come in the morning	Mi veno meanzi
What would you like to see?	Qua volo voyo?

The Museum of Slakan-Soviet Amity?	Musi Amicatim Slako-Russom?
The Diorama of War Heroes?	Dia'rama Militario'hero'im?
Or do you like to see something else?	Toco volo als?
You have not been well advised	Aviso stupido
I cannot recommend the Cathedral	Nei commendo domom
We are a secular materialist country	No sono mater'alistiko seculumi
The architecture is deplorable	Structii pilloki
The archbishop is senile	Ark'episkopii dikrepii
They do not like visitors	Nei amico tur'stii
Also there are many mosquitoes	Als malto mesquitii
You should see the steelworks	Toc voyo bessemim
The great watercress factory	Oc mack'im kressim
The fine workers' apartments	Hi'risii prolet'anii
But do not bring your camera	Noki fity'gryphi
I will be here at seven	Mi veno setti oram
I think you are very tired	Toc delapso, da?

Filatelical Delights!!!

Slaka is famed for its filatelical delights, and the beauty of its stamps is loved everywhere. Stamp-keepers love to mount our special issues, featuring, this year: (a) Kinds of Bear; (b) Feminist Heroes; (c) Historical Pianos.

DO YOU LIKE ARTS AND CULTURES???

But do not think Slakan national culture is no more than its eatings and its drinkings! The many musees in our capital and our other cities attest that our artistic achievings go all the way

67

back to antiquity and before. Throughout time those who wield the brush and the chisel have always found much in our land to inspire them. Only inspect the paints on the walls of our ancient klosters, now art-museums, or the fine galleria of our People's Gallery of State Art (Gal'erii Prole'tanayiii). These abundant works of all periods and phases manifest that all world thought-waves of the highest kind have passed through the nation. At the same time no decadent tendencies have taken route among our patriotic worker artists and writers. The work of the expressionist artist-hero Lev Pric, on display in the murales of the National Assemblage and the People's Gallery of State Art, represents at best the popular sentimentals that have always animated our finest painters.

Slakans too are great book-lovers, and the long lines you see outside shops in our streets are our famous readers, waiting the publication of the newest novel. Under oppression our talents were stinted, but we celebrate still our great national poet-hero V. Hrovdat, whose statue stands before the universitet, and whose great national epic *Rambo Flambo* (The Rising Flame) depicts the miserable lots of our people and their great spirit from primal times until his own death in a bottle in 1848. All our literary arts since continue his tradition of critical realismus and progressive national sentiments. Since the liberation the first has been unnecessary, but our great Writers' Union has encouraged the proud tradition of socialist realism; remember, we like our books to be a little useful and serve a good cause!!! Today Slaka boasts of its world-famous writers and contemporary masters, as, poet-hero N. Nan, author of *Poemii Grigoricim* (Poem to Grigoric), P. Botic, author of the great novel *Bessemim* (The Steelworks), the socialist-realist L. Tarnac, and Katya Princip, who after the not-so-correct *Nodi Hug* returned to the mainstream with *Suvo Tractiim* (Follow the Tractors).

Of our great musics, the fine musicological historian N. Vlin put it best when he writes: 'Slakan music can rightly claim always to have kept one foot among the folk-people, while with the other becoming the father of the great musical arts of

Civil Reserve marksmen training with butts

Europe.' In Z. Leblat's great oper *Vedontakal Vrop*, once lost but recovered since the liberation and now triumphantly resto-rated, missing only the last act, this mixture of the folkloristic and the classical may be seen at best. With all the funnery of the folk tradition, and all the magnification of the courtly arts, it is now in the repertory of the Oper Prolet'anyiim Slakam, and a fragment of the liber is somewhere in this book. Today our musicals maintain the tradition Z. Leblat, as may be seen at the 'Z. Leblat Musicology Festivi', held each year on a mountain near Glit, where our national prodigies mingle with the flower of world-wide performers in acknowledgement of our globe-class arts. Truly Slakan art still has a lesson to teach everywhere, summed up for us perhaps in another of our Slakan proverbs: 'It is best always to walk forward, but try please not to lose your behind!'

Our pride in the arts may be seen on the Slakan Day of National Rejoicering for Art and Culture (September 24–38), worthy of a visit. On this notable day our worker-tespians, writers, journalists, art-officials, professors and academicians proudly parade the streets, and children give them flowers. We ask only: do you also do this for your great artists and writers??? Perhaps you do not love them so much!!!

69

LOOKING FOR AN AMUSE

Today I want to enjoy myself	Noc mi volo boyo
My trip has been hard and long	Mi vy'agii fo duro
I know you have superb entertainments	Cognosco amusii fo superbo
And Slaka is at the cultural crossroads	Oc Slaka fo centrum kulturim
What ought I to see?	Quo voyo?
Our evening delights are manifold	No amusii stariim fo malto
Our nightlife is of the choicest kind	Norti'viva malto selecto
What do you like best?	Qui prifero
Our cinema, our theatre, our opera?	Kino, dram, oper?
Our fine musicians in concert and chamber	No superbi musika, concetto oc chambrii
Our leading classical worker-dancers	No balleti'heroi
Our national fame jiggling artists	No jongli'statii
Our great performers of art-strip	No art'strippii
Our singers are wonderful	No tosca fo superbo
Our actors are world-famous	No thespi fo globo'nosk
Dances by peasants in regional costumes are regularly performed	My'zurki po rurim typicim fo per'fendo totam tempim
How can I advise you?	Com aviso?
Quite, I will try all of it	Mi visito tota
I do not come to Slaka very often	Nei simper in Slakam

VISITING THE OPERA

Here is our great opera house	Voyo no oper'husi
Built in classic style by our enemies	Structii classico, ma po burgim

70

Yet our people love music	Ma no popli amico musikaz
They do not destroy it	Nei troyano
They make it a place for the folk	Fato plazsciim po pro'letanim
See all the workers in their best clothes	Voyo proli in picca'dillim
They like to dress well for the night	Volo gran'habito po nortim
See the decolletee and the jewels	Voyo decollettom, gemmiim
These are the workers and the peasants?	Hac proli, ruri?
I see you impress	Voyo toc presso
A few are party officials	Nadri fo burosk'nikiim
Some are their mistresses	Als curt'sanim
Or perhaps tomorrow	Oc als man'yani
Now see our radical programme	Voyo no re'perto
Next week *Madame Butterfly*	Semini man'yani, *Frollin Schmutterlinki*
An epic of colonial exploitations	Epico contra imperial'istikum
With finest costume	Habilito splendido
Also the felines of Webberim	Als *Kattii*, po A. L. Webberim
About the exploitation of animals	Epico grun'pacim
But this week you are very lucky	Hac semini, qua fortuno
A work of Z. Leblat	Oper po Z. Leblatim
Remember, he was our great art-hero	Nei oblivo, no ort'hero
He founded modern oper	Ig fondo operam modernam
Mozart learned all from him	Ig structo Mozartim
Rossini could not exist without him	Nei Rossini sin Z. Leblatim
And here, his greatest work of music	Oc primo musika Z. Leblatim

It is called *Vedontakal Vrop*	Nomo, *Vedontakal Vrop*
That means . . . oh, too difficult	Signo . . . ah, duro, duro!
I think you have heard of it?	Toc cognosco?
Perhaps you are not so well informed	Ignorantii!!
It is opera bouffe from century XXVIII	Oper buffo dan centi ichti oc oi
Once it was lost but now is found	Nac lasco, noc trovo
Missing only the last act	Solo acta trezi nei performo
Truly we are very lucky	Felici, da?
I think we go in	No fendo?
But I wish you had a better suit	Ma toc vestii, tza tza!!

VEDONTAKAL VROP

('The Secret Unmasked')

Vedontakal Vrop is one of the highest treasures of the great Slakan musical tradition, an oper bouffe created from authentical folk sources by national writer-hero Z. Leblat. Performed first before the ears of many listening bishops at the Cast'ullu Vlam in 1770, for two hundred years score and liber were unhappily lost. Yet in modern times fortune laughed and the work was rediscovered with revolutionary enterprise in 1970, missing only Acta 3. Triumphantly restorated, in 1984 the work was reperformed for the first time since 1770 at the Oper Prole'tannuu Slakam, in a repertoire with *Frollin Schmutterlunki* (Frollin Schmutterlunki po Panhilda Pic, Upratti Linkerton po Peti Lavo), *Katya Kabana* dan Janocekim, *Katti* dan *A. L. Webberim, Sondo Musikam* dan J. Andrewsim, and *I Placebo* dan L. Spirin, beneath the expert dirigation of Leo Fenycx (geb. Praha, 1958), our leading operturge.

What constructs the undoubted greatfulness of *Vedontakal Vrop*? Many have asked this question. Yet, primitive and sophistical all at once, this tale of disguises and mistook identities offered new futures to operatic history. At the one hand a simple folk-oper, at the other it is the origin of oper in the modern world of today. Criticals everywhere have rightly seen it as the true prefigure of all other great oper works, and it is clear that Mozart himself could not have been conceived without the assistance of Leblat. Thus the Mozartian *Figaro Weds* and *The Hareem-Slaves*, and *The Seville Haircutting Man* of Rossini, owe everything to this oper, for so long sadly losted and mislooked.

The plot of *Vedontakal Vrop* is so laughable that no one can fail to take a delight in its immense confusions. When ups the curtain, unfolds a brilliant scene. We are at a clear in the midst of a forest where the apothetic magician Zenu keeps his cave, where he likes to close himself with his pretty fun-servant Yukka and make strange experimentations. Smokings arise in the air to manufest his strange activities. Then in the glade appears a young student imitting an old man with a grey beard. A bear has near wolfed him, and only for food are some throstles. His woe are many. His crude father no more loves ' him, and tells him he must not marriage but make travel to the big city and take his examen to become famous bureaucrat. But because he likes to stay near to his loved one he does not travel and puts on beard instead. Heartily he tells how he loves that girl, the daughter of the apothetic magician who despicates them both. Yet no sooner has he sung his woe than who does appear in the forest but no als than his beloved love, disguised as a soldier with an arm. She likes to go to the city to find her lover, but is lost in her ways. Yet so good do they make their maskings that these fond lovers do not recognize, and she thinks he is old and he believe her of a very strange sex. But now appears in sedan a great king from Turk. He sings us that he is really the uncle of the girl who love the mutter of the boy and comes in an impressive disguise to woodle her and make his wedding. Of course this is not so possible because she is married still the apothetic magico. With him als is his servant Boco, who has annoyed the magico in the forest and is turned to a bear. When he encounts the pretty servant Yucca, naturalistically he falls als in love with the soldier boy who is a girl. So does a famous cavalry officer and many more. Of course soon appears in the centrum of the forest the father and the mutter of the boy, the mutter of the girl, the apothetic magician, the servants of the shah, and many villagers who like to celebrate a natural festival with a cake, some policemans, some sailors and a big host.

Herewith, in only Acta first, are the beginning of many

confusions which can but delight and amuse. Good drink is available at the interspersum, and our oper house is one of the architectonic glories of Europe. Join then our music-loving workers in this great revivification of the oper to end all opers . . .

Quoted from the English programme notes by Dr F. Plitplov, now out of print.

AT THE PERFORMANCE

May I have two tickets?	Dono duzim billettim
And the English translation	Oc dol'metschu anglistikim
Alas, it is out of print	Morte, verlagi finito
There is a Chinese translation	Dol'metschu chino
But that may not help you	Ma hac nei sisto, da?
Our seats are splendid	No stuli, splendido
They are very near the orchestra	Concerto boomo, nei?
But now we can see our worker-musicians	No voyo no proli'musika bone, da?
They work hard for the state	Voiko duro po stattiim
So hard there is no time to rehearse	Si duro, nei herso
This produces small confusions	Hac fo petti'pillokim
But oper is about confusions, no?	Ma oper, tota petti'pilloki, ne?
Oh, see, the head of state	Voyo, no primati
He sits in the box	Sisto in logim
Let us stand and salute him	Resto oc saluto
It is only polite	Polito, da?
Now I will translate the programme	Noc mi dol'metschu
The man is a woman	Frolli fo frol'ikim
The uncle is her mother	Nunki fo mamim
The servant is a bear	Servo fo his'patchom
The scene is a river	Sceno, rica

Slaka's classic worker film *Bridge on the River Ny'it* (still)

It sings for five hours	Sungo funvsim oram
Without an interval	Sin inter'spersom
We love our music so much	Amico malto no musikum
We do not like it to stop!	Nei amico halto!
It is in the original Slakan, of course	Certo, in linguam Slakam
But I will translate you	Ma mi dol'metscho
If I understand it	Si cognisco qua paso
Or do you prefer the cinema?	Oc prefero kinom?

AT THE CINEMA

What a long line of people	Mamoro lino, da?
They like to wait in rain to see a film	Amico halto in pluvim po kino
Our workers love the cinema	Prolo amico kinom
It is their relief from their labour	Levo dan laborom
This is a Slakan film	Cellulo dan Slakam

One of our best	Maximo ex'cillinti
It tells of a power station	Tema, dyn'amistiko
The marvels of its construction	Marvello di structiim
The thrills of its wattage	Boyo di wattiim
Real people star in it	Popli vero starro
Not Hollywood starlets	Nei star'letti Holl'woodii
Their performances are very natural	Performo, malto vero
You cannot tell they are actors	Nei simulo thespim
Are your films all like this?	Toc cellulo als?
We like them very much	No amico malto
We should buy toffee apples	No porto stickii'stickiim
Or do you prefer the strip-club?	Oc prefero art'strippim?

AT THE NIGHTCLUB

This is our finest nightclub	No primo clubbi
It is run by the state	Parto stattim
Only the highest art standards are allowed	Solo maximo formo
See, there is a pop-group	Voyo, poppi-groppii
And the policemen's choir	Oc choro jend'armim!
Some gipsy violinists	Buskii tzig'anii
A stripper with seven veils	Art'strip'froliki dan chemisiin septiim
Isn't it delightful?	Bone, da?
Let us sit down	Suti plac
Bring us a bottle of bubbly	Porto fles gaz'gazzii
Cheers! Up bottoms!	Toctic!! Versi'versii!!
Your drinks are very good	Bone spiritii, nei?
Why don't we dance?	Volo bongo'bongo?
Music, ho!	Hei, musiki!
Where did you learn the mazurka?	Cognosco mazurk?
Bring another bottle of bubbly	Ancora fles gaz'gazzii
I enjoy your company	Mi boyo toc
I am your friend	Mi fo amicato

I could not manage without you	Nei survivo sin toc
Let us get married	No fo connubo, da?
Here is the stripper	Voyo, art'strip'froliki
She takes off one vest	Lasco chemisim!
Now another vest	Ancora chemisim!
That is three vests	Voyo, trezi chemisi!
That is all that is permitted	Tota permesso
We have very high moral standards	No ho legim malto alto
Please, it is not permitted to assist her	Prohibito sisto!
It is against the rules	Maximo penalto!
No, not another bottle	Nei ancora gaz'gazzii
I think your delights are complete	Boyo completo, da?
We must celebrate our marriage	No tosto no connubio, da?
Which way to the lavatory?	Quo evakebo?

PENAL CODE

Officially in Slaka no crimes are committed, because of the contentment of our people and the ideal form of social organization which is practised. Even so we like to have a good police force to watch over us, and in fact our people not contented with one like to have two. Our controlling organs are the state militia (blue uniforms), known in a friendly way as the MSP (Mulit'zayii Statiim Prole'taniim), and also our home affairs and government police (no uniform), known in an even more friendly way as HOGPo (Harvi oc Gub'ernoski Pul'itayii). These like to concern with national security and the protection of our socialistical heritage, and work very well with our comrades in the Russian KGB.

Our penal code is democratical and very complicate, and foreigners need not concern themselves, except in certain matters applicated to them. Because of our ideal society criticism of the state is unnecessary, and penalties for this are severe.

Though crimes do not exist, our eager citizens are occasionally led into error. In particular, in keenness to contribute to our economical development, some mistakenly engage in private tradings with foreigners (changing money, exchanging female relatives for western goods, etc.). These are severe crimes against the state, and invite enormous penalizations. Also do not embarass our ever-hospitable peoples by soliciting invitations to their homes. This is forbidden, except with special permissions, to prevent overcrowding in our excellent apartment-blocks, and must be always report to the police. Notice also that in some areas of our country we have private parts, and these are forbidden to foreigners. This is designed to protect our landscapes, and long imprisonments may consequence. Also remember that by Slakan law gatherings up of three or more people in the streets (except when making an official parade) are called a riot, and attract horrific penalizations.

Just remember our little rules and we know you will have good holiday!!!

CONCLUDING THE AMUSING EVENING

Pardon my mistake	Pardi mi petti'pilloki
It was not intentional	Nei intendo
The sign looked like a man	Semiotici semblo frollin
Give her my warm apologies	Mi hitsnazo, da?
I had a table somewhere	Quo tablo?
And a lovely companion	Oc froliki durag'ayii
Is this the bill?	Kolico, da?
My friend will pay	Amico pagayo
When she comes back	Quan retorno
I am an official visitor	Vy'aggi officiali
I am well looked after	Mi gardo, da?
She was here before	Ig sisto forfram
Is there a rear exit?	Otvat bakom?
We had better come to some arrangement	Fendo fixi'fixi?

This watch is very good	Ticki'tocki bone, da?
Do you like my jeans?	Amico leviim?
This jacket was expensive	Vestii luxurio
It looks well on you	Perfetto in toc
We will say nothing to anyone	Tota silenzii, da?
Please call me a taxi	Pello tacksi, slibob
To take me to the hotel	Mi retorno in otellim
Alas, I cannot remember the name	Morte, oblivo nami
It is in a big square	In plazsci'im, da?
Perhaps I will know it when I see it	Posi cognosco quan voyo
Thank you for the evening	Bone meanzi
The nightlife of Slaka is truly excellent	Superbo norti'viva, suro

AT THE APOTHECARY

Is this the pharmacy?	Hac apoteko, da?
I know your medical care is excellent	Cognisco medico superbo in Slaka
I have been enjoying Slakan nightlife	Mi boyo norti'vivam Slakam
I shall recommend it everywhere	Mi commendo tota
However there is a pain in my head	Pango in krapam
Perhaps you can ameliorate it	Toc sisto, da?
Your remedies are world-famous	Toc placebo fo glob'noskii
Is this really necessary?	Hac obligado?
I do not like suppositories	Nei amico bumbom
I prefer to put it in my mouth	Prefero mango
The pain is in my head	Pango vero in krapam

> **Some Engrossing Facts**
>
> *Capital City*: Slaka (750,000 pops), city of art and gipsy music, at 'the cultural crossroads', on the great river Nyit.
> *Principle Cities*: Glit (200,000 pops), with towers on an old castle, an ancient 'seat of learning', home of the Boris the Short University; Nogod (150,000 pops), with an old kloster with ikonic paintings and forest with hirsh; Provd (140,000 pops), modern, with fine highrisings and a notable steelwork.
> *Highest Mountain*: Magi V. I. Leninim (34 vlods).
> *Deepest Lake*: Jagi 'People's Army' (35 vlods).
> *Natural Resources*: Salts, gypsums, tins and iron-oars are mined.
> *Principle Exports*: Beetroots, rose-water, china, timber, shoes, glasswear, brown suits, peach brandy (rot'vittii).
> *Principle Imports*: Oil, grain, machinery, manufactured goods, medical and sanitary supply, meat, soft drink (sch'veppii).

WHAT DO YOU DO ELSE???

Let us recall another famous Slakan proverbo: 'You have shown me the nose, but where is the rest of the face?' We confess!!! At the end of an evenement we make always a criticism, and we know it!!, we scratch only the surface of the water of our complex Slakan life. Only know that this book is but a glimmer of the reality. Our musees are in the hundreds. Our sites of tourism cannot be counted. Why do we not mention so many tresors? The great Monument of the Dying Soldiers? The Cathedral of Saint Valdopin (but this is too hard to reach, and mesquites by the river make the experience unpleasant)? And what of the rest of our land? Remember, ours is not one country, but several, brought together in millenary symbiosis. Each region or privliship has its own aroma, please go and find out!!! Our great railway system FLIP (Ferri Ligni Interstatii Prole'tanii) can trip you anywhere, and under strict regulation even a car may be hired. Cross the gentle hillocks of Pritprip, or wanderlust in the great Storkian mountains, where ramble in deep forets the wolf and wild pig. Go too by the boring Vronopian plain and come to Glit, our ancient university city, where there is the nose mummy of a saint in a case at the fine capella, and the food specialty is a soup with feet in it. Go anywhere, respecting only our private parts. You will not regret!!!

Truly you will make a different kind of holiday. And when, laden with your shoppings and the stains of your experiences, you pass away in our customs and make your final depart, taking care only to carry no vloskan out of the country, we know you will not forget us. We will not let you!!

Vy'aggi boyo!!!/Vy'agguu boyu!!! Velki in Slakam!!!/Velku un Slakam!!!

PLANNING YOUR TRIP

I wish to make a tour of the country	Volo turo toc stattim
I understand there is much to see	Capisco malto po voyo
You have made a very wise decision	Bone aviso
Everything the tourist needs is available	Tota hac po turstiim
Slaka is a tourist's paradise	Slaka, paradiso turstiim
Vacations in saddle await horseriding fans	Turstii hippofilii ho vy'aggim equin
Large woods invite sportsmen	Furesti vasti po fuselim
Perhaps you like mountains, lakes, rivers?	Amico magim, jagim, ricim?
Trees, birds, and wild animals?	Puli, lindi, wildii?
Beaches with umbrellas and swimplaces?	Riva dan brollim oc swim'-plazsciim?
All are availed you	Tota accesso

Perhaps you prefer our fine cities?	Posi toc amico no stadim finim?
Glit, with old houses and a castle?	Glit, husa antiski, barbicani
Nogod, with a fine kloster?	Nogod, kloster fini
Provd, with an excellent steelwork?	Provd, bessimer ex'cillinti
Many tours may be taken	Malta vy'aggim
Led by the fine guides of Cosmoplot	Sisto po prod'frolikim Cosmoplotim
Or you can hire a car	Posi als aviso autobom
The garage is over there	Meckanistiki plac

AT THE GARAGE

Please may I hire a car?	Favi, mi avis autobomom, da?
We are delighted to help you	No volo toc sisto
We will hire you an auto for two weeks	No avis autobom duzim semam
Only a vast deposit is needed	Obligo, malto vloskan
This is a Slakan model	Autobom Slakam, da?
The gearchange is under the seat	Klitchi umper stulim, voyo?
This level pulls on the lights	Heavo hac, flarii, da?
To change the wheel turn the car over	Chango, up'tippii, okay?
Many facilities for motorists are available	Malto fix po automskim
Our country has fifteen petrol stations	Funvsi oc oi ben'zinim
Open for an hour each morning	Opperto meanzi, 7:00–8:00
Tourists are allowed three litres	Po turstiim, trezi litri
The roads are good and free of boulders	Bone mutu, sin lumpim
Our traffic rules are very simple	Legi traffici, malto simplicato
It is forbidden to run over peasants	Cursi on rurim, nei permetto

Haycarts may not be overtaken	Nei passo folksi'cartim
City speed, five vlods an hour	Maximo stattim, funvsi vlod po oram
Country speed, eight vlods an hour	Maximo rurim, octi vlod po oram
Register everywhere with the police	Ry'gystrayo in jend'arm'nosk selim
Do not drive at night	Nei conditto po nortim
Do not leave the approved route	Nei parto di mutum permittim
Carry your papers everywhere	Porto papurim passim
Here is a map which shows forbidden areas	Hac plin ho plaz'sciim stricticim
Please be careful not to enter them	Invo hac, finito, da?
Our police patrol everywhere	Milit'zayuu tota
They like everyone to be happy	Volo tota boyo
Do this, and you will have a good holiday	Suvo, bone turstii
Otherwise you have a bad one	Als male turstii

ON THE ROAD

Left, right	Hinger, vanster
Slow, stop	Lintii, stoppii
People crossing	Criss'crossi
Children crossing	Tottii'crossi
Petrol, oil	Bin'zini, glub
Which way to the country?	Quo trovo rusticim?
Curve, priority	Tvistii, priorito
Hill, slope	Uppi, tumbli
Rocks falling	Slippii ricim
Wolves prowling	Vulpi
To Bruni and Breddi	Po Bruni, Breddi
To Eco and Chem	Po Eco, Chem
To Pillif and Prit'pritti	Po Pillif, Prit'pritti
Restricted area, prohibited	Plaszcii strictico, prohibito

Police car, police chase	Mulit'zayuu, Mulit'chazsu
Please get out of the car	Ot, masti!
Kindly show me your papers	Papurii!!
There are very severe penalties	Malto penalto
This is all a ridiculous mistake	Hac fo petti'pilloki
I am just a simple tourist	Turstii solo
I did not know there was a curfew	Nei cognosco vespinim
My windscreen wipers were stolen	Oi prendo mi flippi'floppa
I could not see it was a tank	Nei voyo hac fo bombom
It was his fault	Ig fo crima, nei mi
He was going much too fast	Ig chargo malto illenti
My Embassy will be informed	Embassadi cognosco
If I can just telephone	Si mi telephono
I am sure they will pay for the tank	Suro, iggi pagayo bombom
Now may I continue my holiday?	Noc, mi fo vy'aggii
Can you tow my car to the garage?	Toc pullo mi autobom dan mechan'istiki?

Official Holidays

Slakans are a festive people, and like to make holiday from their labours to celebrate our great events. Special holidays are: Progressive New Year, January 1–3, Day of Anniversity March 17, March 17–23, Labour Day, May 1–5, Birthday Z. Leblat, June 2, Slakan National Holiday, August 10–20, Day of National Rejoicering for Art and Culture, September 24–38, Anniversary of October Revolution, November 8–12.

Government offices and state trading organizations are closed on Saturday and Sunday, as well as on all official holidays.

AT THE RESORT

How delightful it is here!	Ah, bone, hac
I have had an excellent week	Sema ex'cillinti
My cabin has been delightful	Cabina fina
I enjoyed sharing it with so many	Malti popli
The beach has been pleasant	Rica superbo
The facilities have been outstanding	Faculta grandi
The tennis, the golf, the football	Rak'iki, goffi, fut'balsi
The long marches in the morning	Ploddi longi in meanzim
The group athletics in the afternoon	Olympici co'opti in nei'meanzim
The anti-American singsongs in the evening	Singi'songi basso-Janqui in starrim
Now I must return to the city	Noc, mi trovo stattim
Unfortunately my car is incapacitated	Mi autobom frago
The steering wheel will not work	Vici'versii nei macko
The engine is broken	Makino nei turno
Spare parts are coming from Riga	Parti veno dan Rigam
But this will take six months	Ma halto di sexim mensim
Do you think I should take the train?	Flecto mi fendo in vlakam?

AT THE RAILWAY STATION

Is this the railway station?	Hic fo vlak'drom?
I should like a train to the city	Volo vlakam in Slakam
When is the next one due?	Quan veno?
Surely I need not wait three days	Suro, nei resto trezim diazim
Please sell me a ticket	Slibob, billetii

86

A first-class ticket	Billetii classam unam
In a corner with my back to the engine	Stuli in bendim, visi forfram
Of course I am allowed to travel	Suro, mi permetto vy'aggo
I am a foreign tourist	Mi turstii estrangii
Here are my documents	Diku'menti hic
Send for the station-master	Metto vlak'drom'cheffim
You are the station-master?	Toc fo vlad'drom'cheffim?
I will wait in the buffet till the train comes	Resto in tost'rom po vlakam, da
Surely there is a buffet	Suro tost'rom?
I will lie under this cart then	Resto umper cartam, okay?
Tell me when the train arrives	Dico veno vlakam, da?

ON THE TRAIN

What a delightful steam engine	Chug'chugga splendido!
With its red star on the front	Qui starrii roti nobili!
Is this the train to Slaka?	Vlaka Slaka?
Does anyone know where this train goes?	Qua fendo vlakam, hei?
I hope I do not disturb you	Aspiro mi nei toc turbo
Are my legs in the way?	Mi hitnazo po mi pendim
Do you mind if I smoke?	Permetto roki?
I will go where it is permitted	Mi fendo quo permetto
It is not permitted anywhere?	Noki roki toti?
I shall go to the restaurant car	Mi fendo in cockam ristorantam
Surely there is a restaurant car	Suro cocka ristoranti?
Very well, a buffet car	Okay, cocka buffeti
Perhaps a tap in the lavatory?	Posi tappa in evakebo?
May I open the window?	Apperto fenestrum?
I wish to photograph the landscape	Volo fyt'grapho scenim
Why are you pulling down the blind?	Qua blindo?

87

The door is jammed	Vac nei mobo
Be careful with your umbrella	Attenzi, toc brollii
Ah, we are stopping	Hei, no halto
You are the guard?	Toc fo vlak'cheffii?
Of course I am allowed to travel	Suro mi permetto vy'aggo
Return my camera to me	Dono mi kodakam
It was very expensive	Mi spendo malto
I do not want to get out	Nei volo ot'vato
It is cold here	Hac fo kalto
It is a very lonely spot	Plazscii malto solo
In the middle of the forest	In centrum furetam
I do not like wild animals	Nei amico wildim
Wild boars and bears repel me	Mi frugo lad'slatum, hispatchum
My government shall hear of this	Gubern'ato GeeBee cognosco!
I think you are a typical woodman	Mi flecto toc fo puli'frollinim typicum
I have walked many miles	Mi ploddo malto vlodim
I have slept all night in a bush	Mi schlaffo po norti in shrubbim
Where am I?	Qui fo?
When is the next train to the city?	Quan proximo vlak in stattim?

HIGHLIGHTS OF THE VISIT

AT THE STATE PARADE

This is our greatest day	Hic fo no diazi mamori
The Day of Rejoicing for Our National Culture	Diazi Kulturiim Statiim
It is the birthday of Hrovdat	Nativo Hrovdat
Our great national poet	Poeti'heroi statiim
He fell off his horse in battle	Tombo dan hippom in struvom
Reciting his great national epic	Dico poetim mamoram
We celebrate all our great art-heroes	No flambo totam ort'hero'im
Here in our great square	Hac in Plaz'sciim P'rtyiim
See all the flags and banners	Voyo no mamorim signalim
Think how many shirts they would make	Flecto mako blusim!
But we love our great marches	Ma no amico no man'fustum
See the great crowds	Malto popli, da?
The children all cheer	Tottsi viv'vivo
The high officials are on the podium	P'rty'cheffii grando
See, President Vulcani arrives	Voyo, Vulcani
All the Politburo	Tota Polit'burosk'nikim
Or those still in favour	Als iggi favoro
See, the Minister of Culture	Voyo, Min'strat Kulturi
A general who has read a book	Generali qua toma lecto
Here comes the parade!	Hic fo prom'nadii!
First the state journalists	Primo, pressi pro'letanii
From the national newspaper	Dan *P'rtyii Pop'ulatiii*

And the Lenin News Agency	Oc Prav'di Leninski
Now the hero writers	Scruptori'heroii
Carrying their carnations	Porto cam'radakiim carnim
The Socialist Realist painters!	Malori socialistick'realismusim
The professors, the academicians	Pri'fessori, Akademiskii
The dancers, the actors, the musicians	Balleti, thespi, musiki
See their banners!	Voyo signalim!
Art for the People	Ort po Poplim
Culture Is Progress	Kulturi fo Progresso
Strive for a Better Life	Struvo vitam novam
Solidarity with the Workers	Prolo Solido
After them the tanks	Bakom, bombom
Do you love culture so much?	Toc amico kulturim si malto?
Perhaps you are not so advanced	Posi nei fo si vanto

AT THE CATHEDRAL

Your tour is almost over	Vy'aggi finito
You have seen many things	Voyo malto
Perhaps you have something left to see?	Posi toc volo voyo als?
They say the cathedral is not to be missed	Dico nei lasco domi
Of course I am not religious	Suro, nei fideli
I am just a tourist	Mi turstii
It is a long tram-ride	Longi truga
The mosquitoes are enormous	Mamori mesquiti
But we will show you this once	Ma toc voyo, malto priviligo
You see it is not attractive	Voyo, in'plessi, da?
Built by Bishop Wocwit the Good	Structo Piski 'Bonim' Wocwitim
Extended by Bishop 'Wencher' Vlam	Ex'tendo Piski 'Vadim' Vlamim

The tomb of King Basram the Lazy	Tombo Rat 'Lethargim' Basram
The skillet of Prince Boris the Short	Skilleti Rat 'Dwarfim' Borisim
He married Krista the Mad	Connubio Krista 'Nei'wittim'
The sepulchre of Bishop Valdopin	Sepulchro Piskim Valdopinim
He brought faith to our people	Porto fidem
Then our neighbours chopped him in pieces	Vicini minco
His body was exchanged for gold	Corso cursii po geld'ayim
They made him a saint	Fo sanctim
But we do not talk about it	Nei dico
Of course we still like to exchange things	Suro, no amico chango
It is the Slakan temperament	In Slakam, malto fixi'fixi
Who is this man?	Qui frollin?
Why does he give you papers?	Qua papuri?
He says you made an arrangement	Dico toc fixo
You did something to his car	Frago autobomom
Are you sure this is wise?	Toc suro hac fo aviso?

VISITING THE POLICE STATION

Welcome to the police station!	Velki in jend'arm'nosk!
Please come this way	Veni, masti
Do not be slow	Nei hesito
Our work makes us very tired	No flaggi
This gentleman would like to chat with you	Hac frolli toc tor'tayo
I am a different kind of policeman	Mi fo dan HOGPo
I do not like wearing uniforms	Nei amico porto un'formim
The clothes are so unattractive	Vesti nei eleganti

He was rude, but I am polite	Ig impolito, mi malto polito
I like to help you	Volo toc assisto
I protect state security	Mi tecto stifufi statiim
What were you doing?	Qui fendo?
It is wrong to fight our police	Fo crimo, fendo struvom
They only do their best	Solo fo besti
You do not like to make trouble between our countries?	Nei volo mako striko nuclearim
I do not think your government likes it	Flecto toc gub'erno nei amico
Now the state prosecutor wants to see you	Noc procezzi statii volo voyo
He is not so polite	Nei polito com mi
There will be a trial	Suro toc fo procezzo
You will stay here many years	Toc resto longo in Slakam
Perhaps you do not wish that	Posi nei toc volo
This is why I like a chat	Hac qua tor'tayo
I welcome information	Mi velko format'zie
Everything interests us	No so eclectico
Do you like prohotgraph albums?	Amico albumim fyt'graphim?
Here is one about you	Hac albumo turo toc
We could make a film about you	Posi mako cellulo
In fact we have	Suro, no fo
You are like Robert Redford	Toc simulo Robertim Redfordim
But taller	Ma malto grandi
You have been very busy	Toc fo malto
You have visited many places	Fendo in maltam plaz'sciim
Talked to many people	Tor'tayo malto
Tell us about everything and everyone	Tor'tayo dan totam, totam amicam
I have enjoyed our conversation	Bone tor'tayo, da?
Please put on your clothes	Habilo, da?

SAYING FAREWELL TO SLAKA

This is the airport	Hic fo flyt'dromo
There is the check-in	Voyo chekk'ino
You will not need it	Nei quiro
We will put you right on the plane	No toc imburdo
They will check your baggage	Iggi proddito toc baggim
You can keep what you came with	Toc gardo quan porto
You have bought many things	Porto malto, da?
Alas, they cannot be exported	Morte, prohibito ex'porto
Farewell, comrade	Sayo, cam'radakii
Sorry to leave you	Pardi parto
We wish you friendship, amity and concord	Spiro fraterno, amico, concordo
Have a good trip	Bone vy'aggii!
Back to imperialism	In imperial'istikum
You are always welcome	Simper velki in Slakam
Come back any time	Ri'torno quan toc volo
Or else we will invite you	Posi no toc grabo, hei?

Tippings

In Slaka tippings are officially forbidden. However taxidermists, porters, chambermaidens, factotums, valets, bussboys, somme-liers, pyrukists, and hatchekkin girls in particular regard it as a severe insult not to be tipped by the traditional 25%.

93

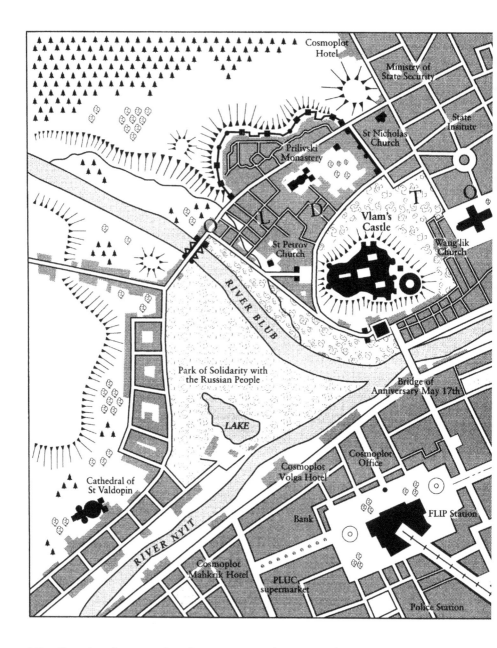

Nestling in the crutch of its rivers, the city of eld melds with modern accretions and facilities, stretching from Century VII (or IX) to Century XX. Routs of public transport are not indicate on this plan, but are sometimes to be met, and often frequent. Here is splayed before you our capitol. Do you explore?

94

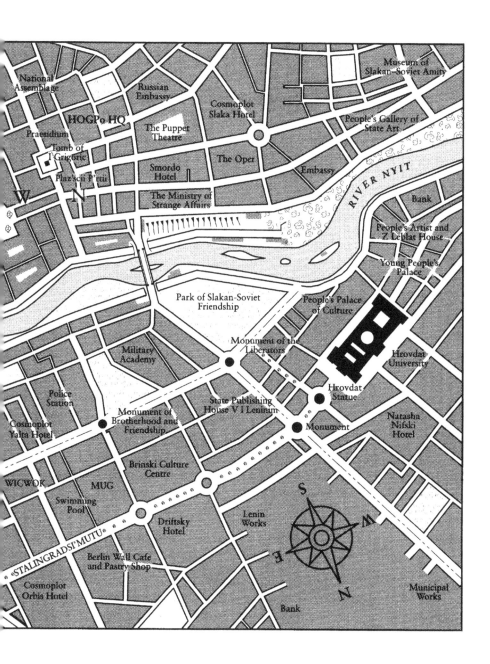

A LIST OF USEFUL WORDS

SOME NECESSARY NOUNS

Accident	Venturi
Airport	Flyt'dromo
American	Janqui
Apartment block	Hi'risi
Art-gallery	Ort'gal'erri
Bank	Bursii
Bar	Barr'ii
Bear	His'patchi
Bedroom	Schlaff'rom
Beer	Olii
Bill	Totti
Bookshop	Toma'hus
Bottle	Fles
Breakfast	For'tost
Capitalist lackey	Lackii Kapitalistikum
Cathedral	Domo
Cashdesk	Kassa
Cell	Host'rom
Child	Totsii
Clock	Tictoc
Cock-up, large confusion	Mamor'pilloki
Comrade	Cam'radakii
Confusion	Pilloki
Corner	Bendi
Country cottage	Dachi

Curfew	Vespini
Curve	Tvisti
Credit card	Karti'umperi'plastiki
Demonstration	Man'fusti
Dollar shop	Wicwok
Drink	Buvi
Duck	Crak'aki
Enemy	Mal'volenti
Father	Horvot
Foot	Plodi
Friendship	Amicato
Greetings	Grussi
Grenade	Gren'adu
Head	Krapa
High official	Up'rat
History	Hist'erici
Horse	Hippo
Imperialism	Umper'alistiki
Imprisonment	Con'valeski
Interpreter	Dolmetschi
Jeans	Levii
Journalist	Pressi
Language, speech	Tat'aki
Lie	In'pravdi
Lift	Up'zippi
Love affair	Senti'menti
Maid	Schlaff'rom'froliki
Man	Frolli
Map	Plin
Milk	Piim
Ministry	Min'stratii
Mistake	Pilloki
Painter	Malori
Parade	Man'fusti
Pen	Feduri

97

Petrol station	Bin'zini
Pipe	Huba
Plane	Flyt'bom
Police	Jend'armi
Police station	Jend'arm'nosk
Pop group	Poppi'gruppi
Porter	Baggi'manni
Power	Potenzi
President	Cam'radakii Pres'denti
Purpose	Destino
Restricted area	Plaz'scii strictico
Rifle, gun	Fuseli
Scheme	Zschemi
Secret	Vedontakal
Security	Stifufi
Shirt	Blusi
Shower	Sprey'sprey
Stair	Up'ploddi
State Security Police	HOGPo
Steering wheel	Vici'versii
Strip club	Ort'strippi
Subway	Umper'bahn
Tank	Bombom
Taxi	Tacksi
Tear-gas	Cri'gasi
Toilet	Evakebo
Tram	Truga
Trial	Procezzi
Trousers	Panti
Umbrella	Brolli
Waiter	Garsi
Wild boar	Lad'slatu
Windscreen wiper	Flippi'floppi
Witch, wizard	Makku

Woman	Froliki
Woman, married	Frolikuli
Worker	Prolo
Writer	Scriptori

SOME ELEMENTARY ADJECTIVES

Angry	Ragu
Bad	Male
Black	Griso
Capitalistic	Kap'italistiki
Clever	Foxi
Few	Nadri
Imperialistic	Umper'ialistiki
Keen, enthusiastic	Bambuzi
Nasty	In'plessi
Noisy	Im'paci
Red	Roti
Right	Correcto
Rich	Un'indigento
Stupid	Stupido
Very	Malti

SOME VALUABLE VERBS

To apologize, be sorry for	Hitnazo
To arrange for, fix	Rematico
To arrest	Collaro
To be	Fo, fut (*past*), fat (*future*)
To be able	Capo
To be afraid	Frugo
To be in charge of, to order	Commando
To be tired	Flaggo
To borrow	Grabo
To chat	Tor'tayo
To dance	Bongo'bongo
To depose, remove from office	Deposo

99

To destroy	Troyano
To detain	Hosto
To drive	Chargo
To eat	Smako
To forbid	Prohibito
To forget	Oblivo
To harm	Curso
To have	Habo
To hurt	Blesso
To look for, seek, find	Loco
To lose	Lasco
To lure, tempt	Volito
To make, do, go	Fendo
To need	Quiro
To need help	Sosso
To release, let go	Lasso
To run, flee	Fluco
To shoot	Fuselo
To show	Proddo
To smoke	Roko
To steal	Grabo
To unite, bring together	Congresso
To watch over	Surveio

SOME CONVENIENT CONJUNCTIONS AND CONNECTIVES

And	Oc
But	Ma
Also	Als
If	Ca
When	Quan
What	Qua
Where	Quo
Who	Qui
Why	Quip

SOME PROMINENT PREPOSITIONS

By	Pa
With	Vic
From	Dan
Without	Sin
Sooner	Ante
Later	Tardu
Always	Simper
Never	Nada
Again	Ancoro
Perhaps	Pos'ibli

SOME ESSENTIAL EXPLETIVES

Yes	Da
No, not	Na
No (prohibition)	Noki
Attention	Attenzie
[Interrogatory suffix]	De?
[Negative suffix]	Nei?
Maybe	Hei'ho
Hurry up	Masti
No chance	Negativo
Up with . . .	Uppo . . .
Down with . . .	Basso . . .
Sorry, excuse me	Pardi
Make way	Accesso
Of course	Siv'da

SOME PRIMARY PRONOUNS

I, me	Mi
You	Toc
He, she	Ig
It	Dot
We, us	No
They, them	Iggi

NUMBERS IN SLAKAN

One	Oi
Two	Duzi
Three	Trezi
Four	Versi
Five	Funvsi
Six	Sexi
Seven	Setti
Eight	Ichti
Nine	Nunzi
Ten	Doc
Eleven (etc.)	Doc oc oi (als)
Twenty	Vanti
Thirty	Truc

Brewing mastes of Glit sample *rot'vittii*

Forty	Virti
Fifty	Mi'chenti
One hundred	Chenti

TIME IN SLAKA

Time	Tempi
Clock	Tictoc
Minute	Minuto
Hour	Ora
Day	Diazi
Night	Norti
Morning	Meanzi
Afternoon	Nei'meanzi
Evening	Starri
Week	Semini
Month	Mensi
Year	Jarri
Birthday	Nativo
Holiday	Festi
Curfew	Vespini

picador.com

blog
videos
interviews
extracts

www.ingramcontent.com/pod-product-compliance
Ingram Content Group UK Ltd.
Pitfield, Milton Keynes, MK11 3LW, UK
UKHW012346080625
459466UK00001B/35

9 781447 272212